ENJOYING MORE
OF LESSER KNOWN
EAST YORKSHIRE

HANDWRITTEN AND
ILLUSTRATED BY
JACK DANBY

Published by Highgate Publications (Beverley) Ltd.
24 Wylies Road, Beverley, HU17 7AP
Telephone (0482) 866826

Printed by B.A. Press, 2-4 Newbegin, Lairgate, Beverley, HU17 8EG
Telephone (0482) 882232

ISBN 0-948929-37-5

British Library Cataloguing in Publication Data
Danby, Jack
   Enjoying more East Yorkshire
   1.   Humberside. East Yorkshire (District) Visitors' guides
   I.   Title
   914.283904859

ISBN 0-948929-38-5

ACKNOWLEDGMENTS

In a score of ways my wife Anita has shared the effort as well as some of the satisfaction of putting these chapters together. As well as taking her usual role of guide, philosopher and friend, she has been driver, picnic provider, literary adviser and resident representative of The Great British Public.

My life-long friend John Moser has been with me on many 'refresher' expeditions into every one of the ten localities I have described. In the course of what John once called our 'companiable questing' we have ridden and walked hundreds of miles together. I have had the benefit of the observations of John's artist's eye as well as the pleasure of his company.

In each locality I have at various times enjoyed conversations with residents. Some have been very helpful. I am especially grateful to Irene and Jack Megginson and Harry Smith of Bishop Wilton, to Elsie and Ivan Evans of Huggate and to Deane and Colin Wigglesworth of Settrington.

I recall also with gratitude the interest shown in my writings by my cycling friend John Hessle, who knew the East Yorkshire countryside so well. Sadly John died before my book was finished. I greatly missed the encouragement of our regular discussions.

I acknowledge with thanks the generosity of the Council of the Yorkshire Dialect Society in allowing me to quote from poems published in their anthologies.

Jack Danby

For
Anita and Carol

especially remembering
their positive thinking
and loving care during
difficult days and nights
in December 1989 and
afterwards

ENJOYING MORE
of lesser known
EAST YORKSHIRE

INTRODUCTION

From the flat fertile fields of Wallingfen to the imposing profiles of the Tabular Hills the East Yorkshire countryside provides a great variety of landscape. The gently undulating plains of Holderness and of the Vale of York, the wide chalklands of the Wolds, the Jurassic hills, the woodlands and the moors all have interesting features for us to enjoy. For this second book describing some of those features I have again chosen ten localities, away from the well known centres of attraction, and have given a chapter to each. My definition of East Yorkshire has little to do with present county or district boundaries; it comprises the whole of the old East Riding and the eastern part of the old North Riding. My localities are not difficult to find but I have tried to help by starting each chapter with a sketch map showing the local roads.

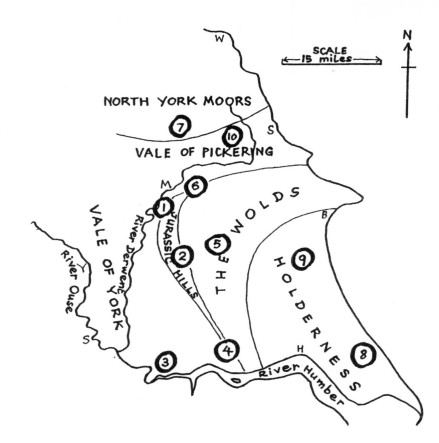

Unless you are a keen cyclist you will need a car for your expeditions; in very few remote places nowadays are the bus or rail services much help. You will need strong footwear too to follow my suggestions, though the paths I think you will enjoy are never very demanding; I have chosen those for strollers and ramblers who have no need to hurry. Occasionally I have inserted a sketch map in the text to help ensure that paths are easy to follow. I have also included below a list of the relevant reference numbers of the O.S. 1:25,000 Pathfinder maps which are useful if you intend to explore these localities on foot, though in some cases I have found that public paths shown on the map, and marked by sign posts and arrows on the site, have fallen into disuse and are difficult to follow. These I have not recommended to you.

The Wolds Way long distance footpath is mentioned several times and to follow any part of it I suggest you use Roger Ratcliffe's book 'The Wolds Way', published for the Countryside Commission by H.M.S.O. in 1982.

In the interval between my writing and your reading about particular people and places there may well have been changes. A housing development, for example, can quickly alter the look of the local landscape and change in some measure the character of a village. Change may be welcomed as progressive or deplored as retrograde. I have described things as I myself have enjoyed them.

O.S. 1:25000 MAPS	
LOCALITY	MAP REF. NOS.
1. THE MIDDLE DERWENT	SE 66/76
2. BISHOP WILTON, BUGTHORPE	SE 65/75, SE 85/95
3. OUSE BANK	SE 62/72, SE 82/92
4. BRANTINGHAM, SOUTH CAVE, NORTH CAVE	SE 82/92, SE 83/93
5. WARTER, HUGGATE, WETWANG	SE 85/95
6. SETTRINGTON, WINTRINGHAM	SE 87/97
7. PICKERING, NEWTONDALE	Outdoor Leisure 27 North York Moors Eastern
8. HILSTON, ROOS, HALSHAM	TA 23/24, TA 22/32
9. WANSFORD TO THE SEA	TA 05/15
10. BROMPTON-BY-SAWDON, WYKEHAM FOREST, TROUTSDALE	Outdoor Leisure 27 North York Moors Eastern

1

HOWSHAM

THE
MIDDLE
DERWENT

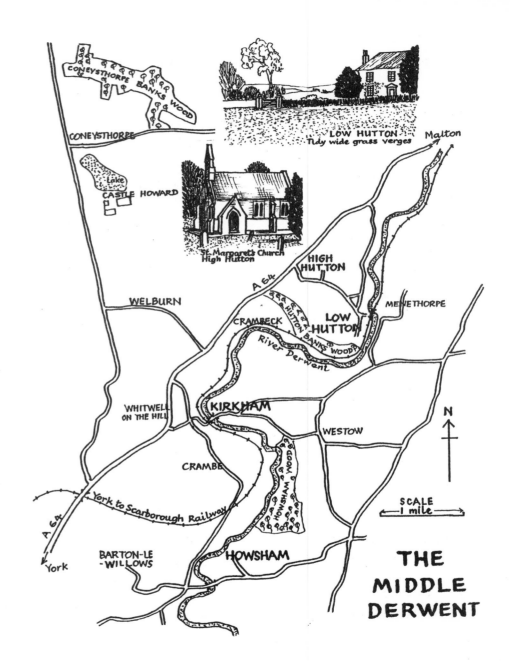

LOW HUTTON
Tidy wide grass verges

St. Margaret's Church
High Hutton

CONEYSTHORPE BANKS WOOD

CONEYSTHORPE

Lake

CASTLE HOWARD

HIGH HUTTON

Malton

WELBURN

A 64

CRAMBECK

LOW HUTTON

MENETHORPE

Hutton Banks Wood

River Derwent

WHITWELL ON THE HILL

KIRKHAM

WESTOW

CRAMBE

Howsham Wood

N

York to Scarborough Railway

A 64

York

BARTON-LE-WILLOWS

HOWSHAM

SCALE
1 mile

THE
MIDDLE
DERWENT

6

THE MIDDLE DERWENT

GLACIAL LAKES OF
NORTH EAST YORKSHIRE

The river Derwent took its present course following the action of the great glaciers. Its previous outlet to the sea near Scalby was blocked by the ice and boulder clay, as was that of the east-flowing river which drained the Vale of Pickering. As the ice gradually receded the melt water formed glacial lakes in which the water-level rose. Hackness Lake overflowed at its southern end and Forge Valley was formed. Water from Lake Pickering found a way out near Kirkham, at the lowest point in the surrounding hills, and took a meandering course south to join the Ouse. It is the area around Kirkham that I have chosen to call the middle Derwent.

If you are not already familiar with the Priory at Kirkham you will probably wish to walk around the ruins, close beside the river. There is convenient parking space near the priory gateway.

The stump of a cross by the gateway to Kirkham Priory reputedly marks the place where the son of Walter D'Espec, the founder of the monastery, was killed by a fall from his horse

The monastery was founded as a house for Augustinian canons about 1125, was later much enlarged and was maintained for four hundred years. The size of the church, nearly as long as Beverley Minster, and of the monastic buildings, was such that they must have dominated the landscape. You get some impression of the scale of the structures just by looking at the remains. After the dissolution in 1540 much of the stone was removed to be used in building dwellings and a new bridge over the river. Howsham Hall, two miles downstream, was constructed partly of stone from the priory and you can still see carved stone blocks in the wall of the farmhouse opposite the gateway which were probably once part of the priory buildings.

Just north of the bridge, arrows on a stile indicate a public path down-river to the west. In fact you can walk on the bank right to Howsham if you wish. It is many years since I went all the way but last July, on a fine morning, we strolled for a mile or so amongst the wild flowers which grow in wonderful profusion along that stretch of the riverside. Great banks of meadowsweet, balsam and a score of other flowers were a delight for the butterflies as well as for us. It seemed that each flowerhead of the yarrow had its own lady-bird lodger, shining in the sun. The bankside alders trailed their lowest branches in the slow-moving water beside the rushes.

If you go that way in summer you may find an angler tucked in amongst the lush undergrowth but more likely you will share the bank only with the wild  creatures. If you hear a distinct 'plop' from the river it could be a water vole (often wrongly called a water rat) leaving its place above the water, disturbed by your presence. There are now a few otters on the Derwent again but you will indeed be very lucky to catch even a glimpse of one.

If you wish to explore the way up-river from Kirkham to Crambeck, go through the grounds of the garden centre just north of the bridge to a point where the path crosses the railway tracks to a concrete stile. Numerous trains use the tracks so obviously great care is needed. You then follow the path arrow signs through the pasture. Again you are unlikely to meet many people. The landscape of this part of the valley is attractive; the railway keeps closely to the course of the river and is not a very noticeable intrusion on the natural beauty. Up to the 1960s there were stations on the line at Kirkham, (called Kirkham Abbey), Crambeck, (Castle Howard) and Low Hutton (Huttons Ambo), but nowadays the York to Scarborough trains stop only at Malton and Seamer. In the 1920s the Leeds fishermen, if they got up early enough, could arrive by train at Kirkham Abbey and be angling in the Derwent by 8 a.m., even on a Sunday.

KIRKHAM

Until well into the 19th century the grassy spaces near Kirkham bridge, and the bridge itself, were used as the site of a locally important Bird Fair, held every Trinity Monday. The tradesmen specialised in the sale of song birds and game birds but there were all kinds of stalls, amusements and refreshments. The local people had a holiday. Frequently, we are told, by the end of the day there were disputes and fights when the young men of Malton took on those from Westoe. These days, beside the bridge, on Trinity or any summertime Monday, you will probably see just a peaceful family group picnicking, an angler or two laden with tackle on the way to a quiet spot and scarcely ever a bout of fisticuffs !

HOWSHAM   War memorial

The attractive dwellings in Howsham village are all on one side of the single street. Houses on the other side were removed about 1770 by the landlord Nathaniel Cholmley who had trees planted in their place. He wished to improve the view of the countryside from his windows in the hall. At that time 'improving' the landscape was fashionable amongst wealthy landowners; it was the time of 'Capability' Brown and his like. So the map of the village looks like this and to this day the view from the hall remains the same.

The hall is now a school. Pevsner describes the south front of the building, which was erected about 1619, as 'one of the sights of the East Riding' and Dr. Allison says 'it is one of the East Riding's brightest jewels of domestic architecture'. You must go and see what you yourself think of it.

Enjoy the village, which always seems to be well looked after. Howsham did in fact win a 'best-kept village' award not so long ago, as the lettering on a well made wooden seat near the footpath in the street, records. The houses are built of the local Jurassic stone, of an attractive colour. The war memorial, the only village memorial I have seen bearing just a solitary name, is a sandstone monolith in the street near the church.

The church of St. John at Howsham was built in 1860 for Hannah Cholmley of Howsham Hall. The architect was G.E. Street.

Howsham Church. West front

Howsham is the birthplace of George Hudson who became famous, or, you may think, notorious, as 'the railway king.' 'Royal George of York' had great drive and determination, great ability in large scale planning, but no regard for the formalities of accounting procedures.

George Hudson was three times Lord Mayor of York and a York street was named after him. You can read an account of his rise and fall in 'Lords of the City' by Charles Kightly and Rachel Semlyen published by York City Council in 1980.

In the railway boom of 1845/6 Hudson misused shareholders' money and had to leave the country in disgrace. He lived the rest of his life, to 1871, in comparative poverty and was buried in his native countryside down river at Scrayingham. (I wonder if Howsham disowned him at the end!)

From Howsham's very solid bridge over the Derwent you can walk north through the pasture and through the riverside woodland to the weir. For nearly two hundred years from about 1740 a water mill, grinding corn, operated here on the village side of the river. A cut, by-passing the weir and the mill, allowed access to a lock for vessels on the Derwent navigation which operated commercially from about the middle of the 18th century until competition from the railways caused its decline a hundred years later and its end in the early part of this century. The Yorkshire Derwent Trust, with Malton Town Council, wishes to restore the navigation up to Malton so that pleasure craft can go up river from Sutton. This proposal is opposed by landowners, farmers, anglers and wildlife conservation interests and is still the subject of litigation.

As one of the very few (and very short) stretches of 'white water' for many miles around, the weir at Howsham attracts canoeists. When I was last there, during the August school holiday, a group of young paddlers was being instructed. The children were  obviously enjoying themselves and the bright orange and red and blues of their craft and costumes gave an air of carnival to the Derwent's pleasant green scenery.

Geographically, Castle Howard is certainly in this middle Derwent area, (I have mentioned that its railway station was right beside the river at Crambeck), but, being nationally and internationally famous, does not belong in my 'lesser known' category, so I am not attempting to describe it. I could, though, direct you to a lesser known viewpoint from which to see the magnificent house and its surrounding landscape. Go north from Howsham bridge through Barton-le-Willows — pausing perhaps to admire the spacious village green and the attractive buildings of local stone and brick — straight over the railway and the main A64 road.

After a few bends in the road you come to a huge monument. This marks the start of an arrow-straight avenue going north for nearly 4 miles. Where the trees end and the road begins to bend you can pull off the road to the right and leave your car. A public path follows a track up to and into Coneysthorpe Banks Wood to the east. From a number of places along the

The monument commemorates George William Frederick Howard 7th Earl of Carlisle 1802-1864 British Statesman Lord Lieutenant of Ireland ridge you can look south across to Castle Howard. Perhaps it was after looking from this high ground that Horace Walpole wrote his much quoted description in 1772 : 'Nobody had informed me that I should at one view see a palace, a town, a fortified city, temples on high places, woods ----vales -----the noblest lawn in the world fenced by half the horizon-----'.

From the path there are good views too in the opposite direction, over the Vale of Pickering. You can turn right down the slopes through the wood to the Malton road from Coneysthorpe, or retrace your steps to the northern end of the great avenue.

Up river from Kirkham and Gambeck the wooded banks of the Derwent mostly rise quite steeply on each side but at one of the lower places is the small village of Low Hutton. Near the site of the old Huttons Ambo railway station a suspension bridge for pedestrians, erected originally, I expect, for the use of rail passengers, provides a way over

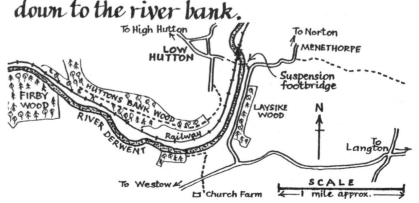

the river to the hamlet of Menethorpe and to Langton beyond. The road from Menethorpe to Westow stays close to the river for half a mile or so, then, about another half mile south, a path, opposite the lane to Church Farm, leads down to the river bank.

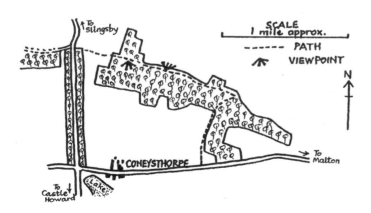

The O.S. map shows the riverside path as 'Giant's Causeway'. It was rough going through the bushes when last I tried to walk along it; (more comfortable for a giant, maybe!) If you decide to go there I am sure you will enjoy the pleasant scene and the quiet. You may also enjoy an occasional brief intrusion on the quietness as you wave to people on a train passing on the north bank.

Low Hutton has fine stone houses and well kept wide grass verges. Near the green is a contrast of ancient and modern; the sombre stone-built pinfold with the bright red telephone booth beside it. I watched a mason repairing the wall of the pound, which is protected by a preservation order but unlikely ever again to be a temporary home for Low Hutton's stray cattle, sheep or pigs.

A track in the south east corner of the village leads down towards the railway and the river, passing some mounds in the pasture on the left which mark the foundations of a mediaeval hall, excavated in the 1950s. The track takes you over an open field into Huttons Bank Wood where you can stroll in the shade. Another path from the village across to the wood on the north side we found obstructed, crops having been sown right up to the hedgerows.

Half a mile north is Low Hutton's sister village with its tidy Victorian church and its imposing Hall. Imposing, that is, if you view it from beside the A64 main road. From the roads in the village the big Georgian house hides behind

a long high stone wall which gives the impression of a fortress. There are old well trimmed yews inside the private drive gates.

2

BISHOP WILTON
BUGTHORPE

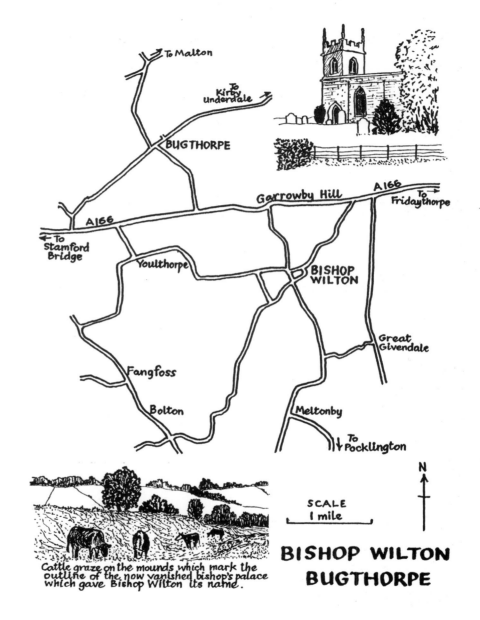

Cattle graze on the mounds which mark the
outline of the now vanished bishop's palace
which gave Bishop Wilton its name.

BISHOP WILTON
BUGTHORPE

BISHOP WILTON
BUGTHORPE

A notable event in the life of many East Yorkshire villages is the annual show. In some places it is a flower or a horticultural show, in some a show for livestock, in others for cookery and other crafts. Often it is a combination of all these with sports and other festivities, too. With the inspiration of a lively committee a village show can go from strength to strength and attract entries and visitors from a wide area. Such a one is Bishop Wilton show. Last year's 92nd annual event had a schedule listing more than 300 classes, a complicated and carefully organised programme and an impressive list of trophies and sponsors. The voluntary work involved in the arrangements must occupy a great many Bishop Wilton people for much of the year. They probably allow themselves an annual sigh of relief when the visitors have all gone and the village returns one summer Sunday morning to its more usual peaceful calm.

You have an impression of peaceful calm if, on a work-a-day morning, you stroll through the village, an impression doubtless helped by the fact that it is impossible for motor traffic to go other than very gently on the narrow beckside roads. The houses

and the farmsteads line both banks of a shallow grassy valley, in the bottom of which runs the beck. The beck is fed by springs a mile or so away at the foot of the wold and flows steadily, but with no great volume of water, even after heavy rain, westward to join the Pocklington beck. There is a house known as Mill House but no evidence, as far as I can see, of the existence of a water mill.

The beck is crossed by footbridges and is taken under the roads through culverts. At one time, up to the 1920s, it was a necessary part of a boy's initiation into the village youth society for him to crawl through all the culverts. A very unpleasant experience, I imagine, looking at the restricted spaces to which the beck is frequently confined.

Close to the crossroads in the middle of the village is the building which once housed the school. It is now part of the premises of an agricultural engineer, who, a few yards away in a window facing the street, displays a 'penny-farthing' bicycle. It has not been ridden for many years but is a reminder of the tremendous changes that have taken place this century. It is not really so very long ago that a 'penny-farthing' was regarded as a dangerous novelty, liable to frighten the carriage horses.

That school building, superseded in the 1860s by the present school at the east end of the village, was also once a meeting place for the local 'court' of the Ancient Order of Foresters, one of the friendly societies established to safeguard the welfare, rights and customs of the working men. In Bishop Wilton the 'court' was in existence right up to the 1970s.

You are likely to find the door of St. Edith's church open and a leaflet inside describing its features and its history. Even on a bright day the interior seems rather dim, as not enough light penetrates the stained glass windows. The beauty of the decorated roof and the unusual mosaic floor cannot really be appreciated without the help of artificial light. The whole interior of the church is kept beautifully clean by the voluntary helpers, some of whom were busy when last I went inside. I was introduced to Eileen Hopper in her home in part of the old vicarage beside the church. She was at work polishing some of the church brass candlesticks, just part of the routine help she has freely given to St. Edith's week by week for well over forty years. That must be some sort of a record!

The restoration of the church in the latter part of the last century was directed by J. L. Pearson who also was the architect of Truro Cathedral. The cost was met by Sir Tatton Sykes of Sledmere whose name is constantly heard throughout the Wolds country in connection not only with church restorations but with the provision of school buildings and other improvements in the villages. There were in fact two Sir Tattons; the first died in 1863 and his son in 1913.

A bust of Sir Tatton Sykes stands in Bishop Wilton church before the window which commemorates his parents.

Benefactors like members of the Sykes family are well commemorated; we seldom hear enough about the Eileen Hoppers of this world.

On the south side of the beck near Mill House a path goes up the wold side to the edge of the woodland. It is a steep climb (though not quite justifying the name of 'cliff' which some local people give it!). Arrows on fence posts show the way across the chalky pasture to the plantation and to the path round the top edge of Old Wood. There are ash trees, beeches and horse chestnuts of splendid maturity; some of very great age. One or two remain standing though they have been dead for years. When I went that way last summer a fine old beech had recently succumbed to a stormy wind and had collapsed across the path.

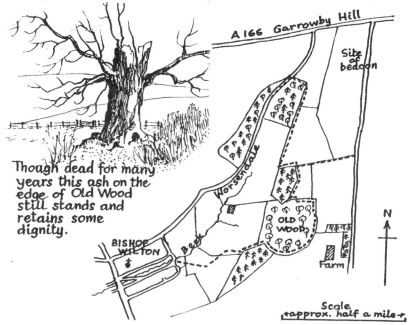

Though dead for many years this ash on the edge of Old Wood still stands and retains some dignity.

When you turn north above the old wood you are going close to the site of Bishop Wilton Beacon, remembered from my own schooldays as, at 808 ft., the highest point in the East Riding. Now that we measure in metres and the East Riding exists only in our memories, perhaps that no longer matters. The beacon was made ready but not lit in 1588 at the time of the threat from the Spanish Armada.

During the Napoleonic wars a beacon tower was prepared again, probably manned by militia men, and may have been lit in October 1803 when the East Riding alarm system was tested. The tower had disappeared by 1850.   From high points on the path above the wood you have a wide view of all the vale and a bird's eye close-up of the village at the bottom of the steep slopes. You can return to the village down Worsendale, —pronounced Wossndill by those who speak our old language—, a more comfortable walk, being gently downhill most of the way.

The O.S. Pathfinder map shows a public path following the beck southwest away from Bishop Wilton village, but after keeping to a farm track for a few hundred yards it disappears into the crops. The course of the beck across the fields is marked by willow trees, some now very old. As you return to the village one huge willow makes a frame for your first view of the houses.

An enjoyable way to spend a sunny hour is to sit on the seat on Bugthorpe village green and watch the rural world go by. It is a busy world, as very few people in the East Yorkshire countryside can afford to be idle during the working week, but, compared to the hectic bustle and noise of traffic in the towns, Bugthorpe is a haven of peace and quiet. And I find any village green a far more interesting place than a crowded holiday beach! Sitting there with your back to the church railings you look past the big sycamore, planted to commemorate King George's silver jubilee in 1935, to the pleasing Victorian brick building at the other end of the green, once the village school but now used as the estate office.

It must have been a magpies' conference day when last I sat on Bugthorpe green. They came in ones and twos from various directions and departed chattering. Splendid creatures! It seems that there has been a rapid increase in the magpie population recently. In my boyhood it was something of an occasion to see just one, and to know the whereabouts of a magpie's nest made me feel important. We used to recite a version of the old jingle which began 'One for sorrow, two for joy---', a superstition which has lingered in my mind.

To explore Bugthorpe village does not take long. That magnificent copper-beech tree near St. Andrew's church is a dominant feature. To see inside the church and to inspect all the curious carvings, you will need to ask Mr. Huffington, at

Lilac Farm over the road, for the key.
The Methodist chapel must surely be one

of the smallest places
of worship in all East
Yorkshire. You will find
it tucked away between
two dwellings on the
north side of the village.
You may like to follow the path
which, just beyond the chapel, takes you
past the gateway to the Old Hall, across
the meadow where the embankments of
an old moat are still plainly visible,
across a footbridge over the beck and up
the slopes to the fields near Thoralby Hall.
It must have been my lucky bird day
when I was there last summer; not only had
I enjoyed the close-up sight of the magpies
but on my way beyond the beck I watched
a pair of little owls, a beautiful bullfinch
in the hawthorn hedge and a group of long-
tailed tits high in the bushes, all in the
space of a few minutes.

The 1/25,000 O.S. map shows the path
continuing beyond Thoralby Hall in a
zig-zag line beside
the hedges of the
undulating fields
to join another one
running east and
west along the line

of the Humberside—North Yorkshire county
boundary. There are arrow signs on posts
and gates but in fact walking is very
difficult as crops are grown right up to
the hedgerows.
On your return towards Bugthorpe
village look closely at the remains of that
moat. Did it at some time have a defensive
purpose? If so, what was being defended?
Or were the embankments just enclosing
fish ponds? I have not yet found an answer.
Near the stile between the moat
pasture and the lane, a pile of sawn logs,
of beech and ash and pine, prepared
against the coming of winter, put me in

mind of that old traditional rhyme about
the burning qualities of different timbers:
  'Beechwood fires are bright and clear
   If the logs are kept a year.
  Chestnut's only good, they say,
   If for long it's laid away,
  But ashwood new or ashwood old
  Is fit for a queen with a crown of gold.

  Birch and fir logs burn too fast
  Blaze up bright and do not last.
  It is by the Irish said
  Hawthorn bakes the sweetest bread.
  Elmwood burns like churchyard mould;
  Even the very flames are cold.
  But ashwood green and ashwood brown
  Is fit for a queen with a golden crown.

Poplar gives a bitter smoke
Fills your eyes and makes you choke.
Apple wood will scent your room
With an incense like perfume.
Oaken logs if dry and old
Will keep away the winter cold,
But ashwood wet and ashwood dry
A king shall warm his slippers by.'

   In praise of ashwood. It would
please me to claim an East Yorkshire
origin for that anonymous poem but I
think it came from Devon. I wonder what
proportion of ashwood was in the log pile
I saw at Bugthorpe; sufficient, I hope, to
keep the sawyer's slippers comfortable.
   You could perhaps go home from
Bugthorpe by the undulating winding road up
to Kirby Underdale which takes you through
some of the pleasantest countryside in all the
county. There are places where you can pull
off the road to enjoy the views and several
public paths if you feel like walking again.

3

OUSE BANK
HOWDENDYKE
TO
FAXFLEET

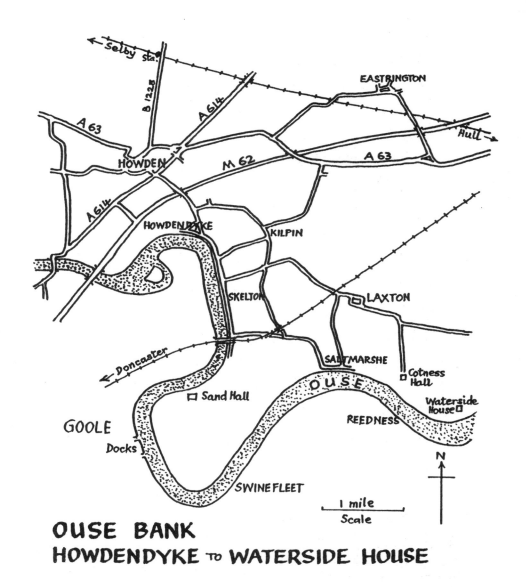

OUSE BANK
HOWDENDYKE TO WATERSIDE HOUSE

OUSE BANK
HOWDENDYKE TO FAXFLEET

"It's a bit like a meeting of the United Nations in here sometimes – half a dozen languages being spoken at the same time!" So said the landlord of The Jolly Sailor inn at Howdendyke, telling me about the crewmen on the ships that come up the Ouse to discharge their timber and steel and chemicals at the nearby wharfs. They are big ships, up to 2500 tons, registered mostly at European ports and manned by sailors of various races and many nationalities. Howdendyke has become a very active inland port, as you can readily see for yourself by walking past the great ware-houses to the river bank.

To watch the coming and going of the ships you need to be there about the time of the turning of the tide. The sheer size of the vessels astonishes me. West of the industrial complex you can walk along the river bank as far as you like. To your left is the wide expanse of the water encircling Howdendyke Island and ahead, a mile or so away, the traffic hurries across the M 62 bridge.

It is only in my lifetime that the Ouse below Selby has been bridged for road traffic; the Boothferry bridge was opened in 1929 and the motorway bridge about 50 years later. The ferry at Booth was much used before 1929 and there were, in use for varying periods up to the early years of this century, ferries also at Newhay, Long

Drax, Howdendyke, Swinefleet, Saltmarshe and Whitgift. Last time we visited Howdendyke we went in search of any remaining signs of the ferry and found them, not surprisingly, at the end of Ferry Road. Amongst the undergrowth on the bank was an old post on which hung a lifebelt marked  FERRY BUOY and a length of hemp hawser. The ferry boat probably crossed to Hook on a diagonal course, taking advantage of the sweep of the appropriate tides. You can see the remains of wharf timbers and a landing place on the opposite bank down-stream. One of the illustrations in Baron F. Duckham's fine book 'The Yorkshire Ouse' (David and Charles 1967) is a reproduction of a photograph taken in the 1880s of the laden ferry boat at Howdendyke. A cart piled high with barrels, with a horse and horseman,

seems to me to form a very precarious load for the rather flimsy craft, but it would not be at all unusual. Stand and look for a minute at the flow of the tide and imagine rowing across in choppy conditions with a contrary wind. It would need considerable skill.

Having refreshed yourself at The Jolly Sailor on the way to Skelton you can enjoy a walk on the river bank south to the Hook railway bridge, or use the road which runs immediately beside the bank. When this bridge was erected in 1869 to carry the Doncaster to Hull railway over the river, which is 770 ft. wide at this point, it was the second largest double line swing

RAILWAY SWING BRIDGE
HOOK — SKELTON

THIS FIXED SPAN WAS BADLY DAMAGED
BY A SHIP IN LATE 1988

bridge in the world. (Tantalisingly I haven't yet found out which was the biggest!) There are five fixed spans, each 116 ft. long, and one swinging span which is 250 ft. long. The swinging part weighs 670 tons and revolves on conical rollers, hydraulically operated. It can be opened in less than a minute and allows ships to use either of two 95 ft. channels. This proved to be inadequate for one navigator in late 1988 and he directed his vessel into one of the fixed spans, causing damage which prevented the use of the bridge by rail traffic for very many months.

The public road goes east from near the railway bridge to Saltmarshe and a private road leads south to Sandhall. The public footpath continues along the river bank and again you can go as far as your energy and inclination allow; all the four or five miles round the great horse shoe bend in the river to Saltmarshe if you wish. If you are lucky in having a fine clear day it is a very enjoyable way to spend an hour or two. There are lovely sycamore, oak and ash trees lining the bank near Sandhall. unobstructed views of the countryside all around, traffic on the river and business at the Goole docks to lend interest. Horses and cattle graze in Sandhall Park. The quiet is seldom disturbed. Close to the splendid buildings of Sandhall is a cherry orchard and an interesting estate timber yard near the bank footpath. When we walked this way last May we paused to watch wrens which had a nest amongst the logs and then, just beyond the yard, I was delighted to see, close to a riverside house, the laundry spread out to dry over the garden hedge in the old-fashioned style.

I was reminded of the East Yorkshire name for a wooden clothes horse; wintredge

The road from Skelton to Saltmarshe takes you through Saltmarshe Park, past the Hall and back to the river bank at the west end of the village.

Saltmarshe Hall was built about 1820. Pevsner describes it as of 'fine ashlar masonry. Two storeys, five bays. Entrance porch semi-circular with Tuscan pillars and columns.'
The Saltmarshe family first owned land here in Norman times.

Again there are fine trees to enjoy and, in the park, numbers of recently planted chestnuts which will ensure enjoyment by succeeding generations too.

From the other end of the village a public footpath leads across the fields to Cotness Hall. Beyond there the path beside the crops is difficult to follow. To reach the river bank top path again it is better to turn right before getting to Cotness Hall and follow the course of Laxton Drain to the river where new sluice gates have recently been installed. The engineers were busy when last we went that way; we thought the mechanical diggers were in danger of sliding into the water but the operators seemed to be entirely at ease.

The confluence of the drainage channel with the river is known as a clough, pronounced to rhyme with bough, not with cough or dough or rough or through (though your dictionary probably tells you to say kluf. We are a contrary lot in East Yorkshire!) From Laxton Clough to Metham Clough near Waterside House is a little over a mile, an exhilarating walk on a fine day in a gentle breeze but not so enjoyable in driving rain or bad visibility. Near Metham Clough, I believe, is the site of the landing place of the Whitgift ferry. Across the river is the jetty, still apparently in reasonable condition, regularly used, no doubt, when the steam packets sailed between Selby and Hull. I think the south side landing place was not far from the jetty. Take your binoculars if you walk along this stretch of the bank and see if you can make out anything strange about the clock face on Whitgift church.

The clock face has XIII instead of XII. The story is that the painter spent too long in the nearby inn and lost count. Evidently the clock was painted in 1919 and the XIII was still there ten years ago. I expect it still is, though my binoculars were not powerful enough to confirm it for me when I looked from the north bank recently.

Your binoculars will help you also to enjoy the sight of all the birds; there will be many pairs of those splendid creatures the shelduck.

John Wesley, founder of Methodism, lived at Epworth in Lincolnshire and often preached in the East Riding, travelling hundreds of miles on horseback. He and his companions used the Whitgift ferry and

in May 1753 he recorded in his diary how, after a visit to Pocklington, they were forced to leave the horses behind, having failed in very heavy rain to get them aboard the ferry boat. I expect the road to the ferry in those days would be by Metham Hall. There is still a public path from Waterside House to Yokefleet but it does not appear to be the remnants of a well defined track that surely would have led to a much used ferry.

Laxton village is a mile or so north from Saltmarshe, a pleasant very peaceful place. There are two churches, the old one having been replaced in 1875 by the church of St. Peter across the road. Only the

chancel remains of the old one but the old churchyard is still the village cemetery.

I usually find something of interest in an old graveyard. A bit morbid, you may think, peering at old headstones, studying inscriptions about people long since dead, but I tell myself that if those who are commemorated in all the epitaphs and memorials could see that someone is taking an interest in them, however belated, they would be quite pleased. Often an inscription can be revealing and interesting. It can be distressing, as when one reads of the death of children. Just occasionally it can be amusing, as the writer of the memorial intended it to be, as, for instance, by making a pun on a name. Not infrequently one wonders about the sincerity of the writers of flattering epitaphs and is reminded that 'the tombstone is about the only thing that can stand upright and lie on its face at the same time.'

At Laxton I was intrigued by the different styles of carved lettering. Beneath an old yew tree and forming the pavement round to the west door of the old church are a number of gravestones of people who died in the 18th century. The lettering on these, something like this:

departed this Life
on the 10th of Novembr
Ano Domi 1749
Aged 67 years

is different from that of a century later when this type of sentimental verse was in the fashion:

Farewell dear Wife my life is past,
To you so long my love did last,
In love we liv'd in peace I died;
Life was desir'd but God denied,
Therefore dear friends contented be,
Prepare in time to follow me.

The association of the yew tree with churchyards dates from the time when congregations met beneath its shade and shelter, before parish churches were built. Even in pre-Christian days the yew tree was venerated. It has a very long natural life-span and is discouraged in places where

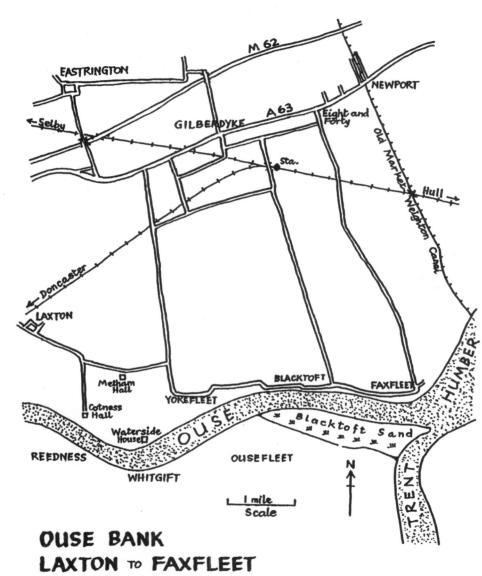

EASTRINGTON

M 62

NEWPORT

←Selby

GILBERDYKE

A 63

Eight and Forty

Sta.

Hull ↑↑

Old Market Weighton Canal

←Doncaster

LAXTON

Metham Hall

YOKEFLEET

BLACKTOFT

FAXFLEET

Cotness Hall

HUMBER

Waterside House

OUSE

Blacktoft Sand

REEDNESS

OUSEFLEET

WHITGIFT

TRENT

N↑

├─ 1 mile ─┤
Scale

**OUSE BANK
LAXTON TO FAXFLEET**

animals could browse on its toxic foliage, so perhaps a churchyard offers the best chance of a long undisturbed life. There are also weeping ash trees at Laxton, planted about a century ago. Perhaps the Victorians thought that weeping ashes were appropriate for a graveyard.

Yokefleet is a 'street' village, farmsteads and houses strung along both sides of a single street, more or less parallel with the river, with Yokefleet Hall hidden in a patch of woodland at the eastern end. Where the road turns north, west of the village, there is a bridge over the wide deep warping drain, giving access to a dwelling and to a path which you can follow by the field hedges to Waterside House.

Stand on the bridge for a few minutes and you are sure to see mallards, coots, moorhens and quite probably a heron. No longer is the drain used for warping (the name given to the process by which the river's high tides were allowed to flood the land, be retained within the sluice gates until the silt they carried was deposited and then be released on the ebb) but several of the main Wallingfen drains are still shown on the map as warping drains. Many years of warping, drainage and cultivation have resulted in highly productive farmland over most of the area which was originally marsh. The Yokefleet warping drain is particularly deep and wide.

seen from Blacktoft Clough
the wharf appears like
a long low vessel
beyond the reed beds

About a mile to the east the Blacktoft warping drain joins the river not far from the wharf where ships are sometimes moored waiting for the appropriate state of the tide before proceeding. I suppose the wharf, or its predecessor erected in 1875, was especially useful for sailing vessels. Negotiating the river, with its banks and bends and variable flow, must be difficult even for the modern powered craft and I marvel at the skill of the old navigators using only the wind and the tide. There were still a few commercial keels and sloops left in the 1930s. The biggest sailing ship ever to get up the Ouse was the grain windjammer Archibald Russell (over 2000 tons), interned at Hull on the outbreak of war in 1939 and towed up to Goole where it remained as a store ship for most of the war years. Late in the last century customs officials were concerned about craft loading and unloading at Blacktoft while waiting for the tides but, as far as I know, no-one was ever arrested for smuggling.

Across the river from the wharf, about a quarter of a mile away as the crow flies but something like eighteen miles by road, is Blacktoft Sand, several hundred acres of reedbeds and marshland, which is an important bird reserve managed by the R.S.P.B. The eastern end of Blacktoft Sand has the Ouse on one side and the Trent on the other. When you reach Faxfleet you are no longer on the Ouse bank but on the Humber. As you go along the road from Blacktoft, past Thornton Lands (once the property of the canons of Thornton Abbey in Lincolnshire)

look at the reedbeds and ponds between road and river. Swans nest there and you will surely see a great many other water birds. A great crested grebe was diving when we were last there.

There was a settlement at Faxfleet in Romano-British times, owing its existence to the use of the river as a thoroughfare, but it was abandoned after serious flooding in the fourth century A.D. The present village consists

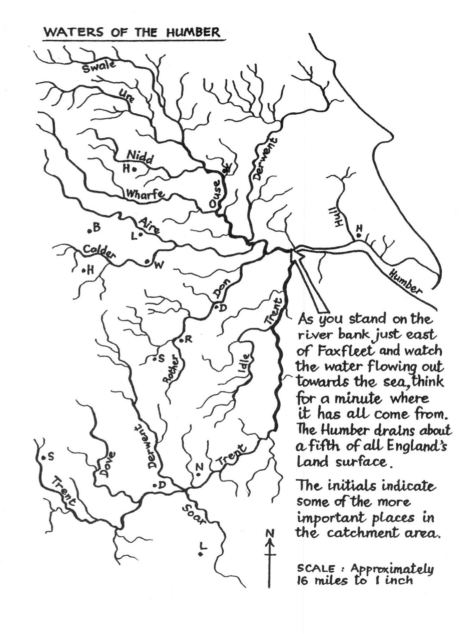

WATERS OF THE HUMBER

As you stand on the river bank just east of Faxfleet and watch the water flowing out towards the sea, think for a minute where it has all come from. The Humber drains about a fifth of all England's land surface.

The initials indicate some of the more important places in the catchment area.

N

SCALE : Approximately 16 miles to 1 inch

of just two farmsteads and their associated dwellings. It is remote and very peaceful. I suggest you find time to walk along the riverside path east to Weighton Lock where the Market Weighton canal joins the Humber. The canal is no longer used commercially but is important as a drainage channel.

As you go, enjoy the openness of the landscape, the richness of the cornlands, the Wolds rising in the distance before you, the slim line of the Humber bridge on the eastern horizon and the wide expanse of the Whitton Sand wildfowl refuge, with the shipping channel beyond, beneath the slopes of the south bank. Whitton Sand is a sanctuary for wintering pink footed grey geese which nest in Greenland, Iceland and Spitzbergen and move south after rearing their young. They roost in large flocks and leave the estuary to graze on the grasslands and the cultivated areas of the wolds. As they fly high, often in a V formation, in the dusk of a November evening, you are more likely to hear their calling than you are to see them. Centuries ago the East Yorkshire countryman listened with real fear to the shrill medley of the calling geese above him. 'Gabriel's ratchets' was his name for them. There was a belief that Gabriel was leading his hounds across the sky hunting for the souls of the dead, he having been condemned to follow the hounds until Judgment Day for the sin of having hunted on earth on the sabbath. To hear 'Gabriel's ratchets' was a sure omen of death. People in the towns and villages near the Humber nowadays will be familiar with the sound, I am sure, but the superstition is almost forgotten.

Faxfleet is at the eastern end of our Ouse Bank wanderings. From there the road goes north across Wallingfen to Newport on the main road to Hull or to the west. The map shows that the area between Gilberdyke and Newport is called Eight and Forty. This was the name given to the building erected, some years before the 1777 act of enclosure affecting Wallingfen, as a meeting place for the delegates from the 48 townships of the area, each of which was represented on the body which allocated rights of stray and settled the other affairs of the fen before the enclosures. The building, very much altered and modernised, is still there and has the name Eight and Forty on its wrought iron gates. I cannot imagine that it was ever big enough for a meeting of 48 people. The occupant tells us he has endless trouble when asked to give his address : Eight and Forty, Main Road, Gilberdyke, and is often told "You mean No.48"

—which he doesn't.

About 20 years ago when I was learning more about East Yorkshire folk lore, asking questions about 'witches and wizards, long tailed buzzards and lizards and sike like things what crawls aboot i dykes at neet' from which the countryman prayed to be delivered, a Newport resident wrote down for me from memory a rhyme which began:

'We're eight and forty jolly girls
Though witches we may be.
We live upon the best of food
And, like the air, it's free.
A moorhen, coot or leveret,
A duck or good fat hen
Each day we're almost sure to get
Around old Wallingfen. '

It is a mystery how the 48 good men and true of the local judiciary were transformed into witches, however jolly and benevolent. Or did each township have a resident witch as well as an appointed delegate?

4

BRANTINGHAM
SOUTH CAVE
NORTH CAVE

All Saints Church
North Cave

Blocked tunnel entrance in Weedley Dale

South Cave Castle Hotel

**BRANTINGHAM
SOUTH CAVE
NORTH CAVE**

BRANTINGHAM, SOUTH CAVE, NORTH CAVE

Brantingham

Close beside the crossroads on the fringe of Brantingham village is the Triton Inn. The triton, in Greek mythology a creature half human, half fish, is the emblem of the influential Sykes family of Sledmere and an indication that the prosperity of their Hull merchant forbears came from commerce on the sea. Look at the gable end of the inn, an interesting

combination of stone-masonry and brickwork. The sandstone comes from a local quarry as Brantingham sits at a point where the chalk of the Wolds gives way to a narrow strip of exposed Jurassic stone and then to the alluvial deposits of Wallingfen. You will notice a great many examples of this kind of brick-work, described sometimes as 'tumbled-in', hereabouts. Perhaps it marked the particular style of a local Georgian or early Victorian builder. I find it attractive.

Across the road from The Triton is Brantingham's war memorial, described by Pevsner as 'one of the most lovably awful things in the East Riding'. The 'awful' I can understand. There is nothing lovable about the monument as far as I can see though there is something to be pleased about in the dignity of the fine lettering on the bronze plaque commemorating the seventeen Brantingham men who died in the 1914 – 1918 war. To see the long lists of names of those killed in

that war and the shorter lists of my
contemporaries killed in the second world
war, on any memorial tablet, fills me with
strong feelings of anger as well as of sorrow.
How can mankind be so stupid as to resort
to mass violence so often? What a terrible
unnecessary waste! Lines from a poem of
Siegfried Sassoon's often come into my mind:
    'You smug faced crowds with kindling eye
    Who cheer when soldier lads march by
    Sneak home and pray you'll never know
    The hell where youth and laughter go.'
Wilfred Owen wrote that if those who preach
about 'the glorious dead' could see the horrible
obscenities of death in the muck of the battle-
fields they would no longer
        '..... tell with such high zest
    To children ardent for some desperate glory
    The old lie: dulce et decorum est
    Pro patria mori.'
        [It is a sweet and proper thing to die for the fatherland]
Looking at any war memorial also makes me
remember the East Yorkshire dialect verses

of Q. Nicholas:
    'When of a Sunda Ah sits i mi pew
    Ah sees a list o lads at yance Ah knew
    An then it ardlins seems a day sin last
    Ah spooak tiv em, though monny years es passed.

    There's Dick, at were a champion wi t ploo
    Ti set a rig an furrow stright an true,
    An Ben, at snickled monny a fine fat hare!
    E'll nivver trouble t keepers onny mair!

    Arry, at oor Sarah used ti cooart,
    An Bob at were a dab at ivvry spooart.
    When Ah were young Ah palled on wi em all—
    Bud noo they're nobbut neeams upon t choch wall.'

Q. Nicholas is the pen name of an East Yorkshire
man about whom, I regret to say, I know nothing.
        The Brantingham war memorial
was put together from bits and pieces retained
when the Victorian town hall at Hull was
replaced by the new Guildhall in 1916. From
the same source came the stone urns which

you can see on gate-posts near the memorial and near the village pond. It is a pleasant experience to sit near  the pond on a spring day and watch the ducks. In mid-April last year there were scores of baby mallards, just a few days old and apparently independent of their parents, wandering about. They seemed very vulnerable. I wonder if the Brantingham cats are specially trained to ignore them!

There are some well-built houses and fine trees clustering around the village green and a stroll along the narrow roads is a rewarding experience.

 All Saints' Church at Brantingham, of ancient foundation but largely restored in the 1870s, sits on the side of the dale just north of the village against a background of woodland.

The sandstone wall surrounding the church-yard was being rebuilt when we were there recently. The great concrete slabs with which it had been previously, and quite unsuitably, capped were being replaced  with sandstone pavers. The mason in charge explained the structure, with a section like

this   rather than which is usual in the dales of north west Yorkshire where stone walls form most of the field boundaries. To watch good craftsmen at work is always a pleasure. When you go that way stop and see how the finished job looks.

Close beside the church the Wolds Way footpath from the east joins the road and follows it up Brantingham Dale for about half a mile before turning left on a track through the woodland. This is an enjoyable way to go to South Cave so maybe you could make your transport arrangements accordingly, put on your strong footwear and have a pleasant stroll over the top of the Mount Airy wold. The way is well sign posted but this sketch map may be helpful.

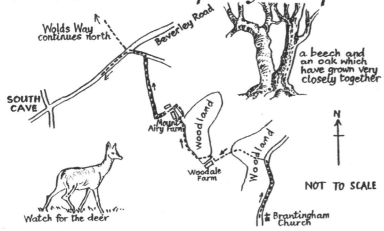

The numerous footpaths in the area are well frequented at weekends, especially in summer, by people enjoying the countryside, but on weekdays you will probably have the path to yourself. Watch for the deer, though your chances of seeing them are slight; they know of your presence long before you suspect theirs. Other creatures you will certainly

see, especially birds. The way goes quite steeply up and down; no bother for younger walkers but others will want to go gently. There are beautiful beech trees close to Mount Airy Farm. As you approach the buildings look for a beech and an oak which have grown together all their lives in such a close embrace that they appear to have a common root system. They are readily recognised because many years ago children built a tree house in their branches and a few strong planks are still there.   The track down from Mount Airy joins the Beverley road to the east of South Cave and you turn left into the village.

We think of South Cave as a village but until comparatively recently it enjoyed the status of a town, mainly on account of its weekly market and its two annual fairs, held, my 1840 directory tells me, on Trinity Monday and Tuesday and on the second Monday after old Michaelmas Day. The market hall was built in 1796 and about 50 years later was described as 'a neat edifice of brick with an arcade on the basement, a schoolroom above and on the top a small circular bell-turret, in which is a good clock? That clock was replaced in 1887 in celebration of Queen Victoria's golden jubilee and has recently been renovated.

Not far from the market hall is the Fox and Coney inn from which in the 1830s mail coaches left at 6 each morning for Sheffield and at 6 each evening for Hull. There was a daily service to Selby and from The Bear across the road coaches went regularly to Wakefield. The Hull and Selby Railway, opened in 1840 with a station at Brough, no doubt changed the habits of the South Cave travellers and then, in July 1885, they got their own station on the Hull and Barnsley Railway. It is now about 30 years since passenger trains called at

South Cave station and the rails have long since been removed. The cuttings in Weedley Dale, once noisy with the bustling of the freight locomotives, now provide the track of a very pleasant walk to enjoy the quiet.

The main freight was coal to and timber from the Hull docks

A feature of the locomotives built for the Hull and Barnsley Railway was the domeless boiler.

Have a look at the sketch map on the next page and choose a way to get from the village to Weedley Dale. The lane from the quarries has been much used lately by huge trucks bringing stone to change the face of the landscape where a new golf course is being created, so you may prefer to avoid it. The public paths are well defined. You can walk on the old railway as far east as the brick viaduct which was originally built for farm traffic near the tunnel entrance but which obviously

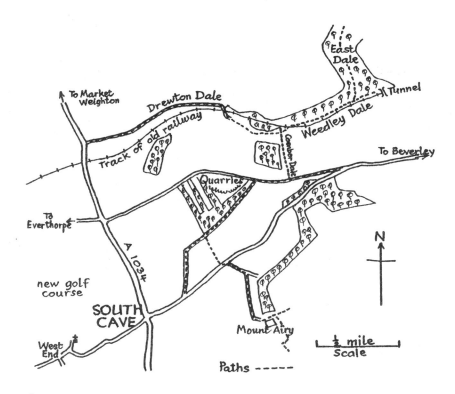

has not been used at all for many years. The brick arches, set askew, are cleverly constructed but now beginning to crumble.

Listen to the birds. When, last April, we walked that way, a thrush was in full song high in a larch tree at the edge of the plantation bordering the cutting and, to our delight, the flowers on the tree below him glowed a glorious pink. We could have had

no better illustration for Wordsworth's lines about March:

'... when rosy plumelets tuft the larch And rarely pipes the mounted thrush' Except, of course, that it was April! March is usually rather early for the rosy plumelets.

The original village of South Cave was in the area near the church, half a mile or so west of the market hall. Between the two parts of the village is a small lake in the grounds of Cave Castle, built in 1804 for a Hull merchant, much altered since and now a hotel. In South Cave West Hall, a building which I cannot identify and which may well have now disappeared, was born John Washington, great grandfather of George, 'founder of the American republic', who emigrated to Virginia in 1657.

The church of All Saints has been there since mediaeval times but was largely rebuilt in the 1840s. The clock is modern and commemorates Queen Elizabeth's 1977

Close to the church Cave Castle Hotel has an ornate arched entrance with a castellated lodge

silver jubilee, installed 'by public subscription and endeavour.' There are no numbers on the clock face but it is admirably clear and simple.

In the 1540s, in the course of his travels helping to list the assets acquired by Henry VIII on the dissolution of East Yorkshire monasteries, John Leland approached North Cave 'from Walkington V miles by fair champain corn ground' and recorded in his Itinerary 'there rennith a broke by North Cave and so into Humbre.' The broke still rennith. It was being enjoyed by a whole flock of ducks when we walked beside it recently and we thought how pleasant to have a garden running down to its bank, as many North Cave residents have. Over the centuries that brook provided the power for three mills and so was of prime importance in the life of the village. The mills no longer function but, as a reminder, mill stones have been built into the garden wall of Mill House and, if you walk that way, along the path which takes you over the stream to Nordam, the village's northern street, you can still see where the head of water was built up and the mill wheel turned.

North Cave is full of interesting buildings, many dating from the eighteenth century. As in Brantingham and South Cave the builders had ready access to sandstone and chalk as well as brick so frequently you find an intriguing mixture. Wander around, not only by the stream but along the streets and by the church, and see how old and new buildings have been very happily blended together. There are lovely trees, too. Sadly one of the big beeches near the church was being felled when I was there recently. Being in a dangerous condition close to the main road and close to buildings, it had  to come down piecemeal. Although I love the sight and texture of seasoned timber of beech or oak or ash I find something disturbing and dramatic about the end of a full grown tree. Decades, centuries even, of growth and maturing are suddenly finished in a brief onslaught of saw and axe.

Just east of the church, which you will probably find locked, is the fascinating group of buildings of Manor Farm, built of sandstone and brick about 1770 and including an octagonal dovecote.

If you are not yet weary of walking you might like to follow the path along an avenue of trees from Nordam towards Hotham. It is very pleasant, running more or less parallel with the private road to Hotham Hall. Before you leave Nordam have a look at the painted notice fixed to the renovated lodge at the entrance to Hotham Hall Park. Having survived the slaughter, which took the lives of scores of his own friends and fellows, the colonel evidently wanted posterity to be reminded of the horrendous scale of the sacrifice. His statistics underline the comments I made at Brantingham.

To YPRES
347 miles
In defending the Salient our casualties were
90,000 killed
71,000 missing
410,000 wounded
Erected by the late
Col. T.C. Clitherow DSO

5

HUGGATE

WARTER
HUGGATE
WETWANG

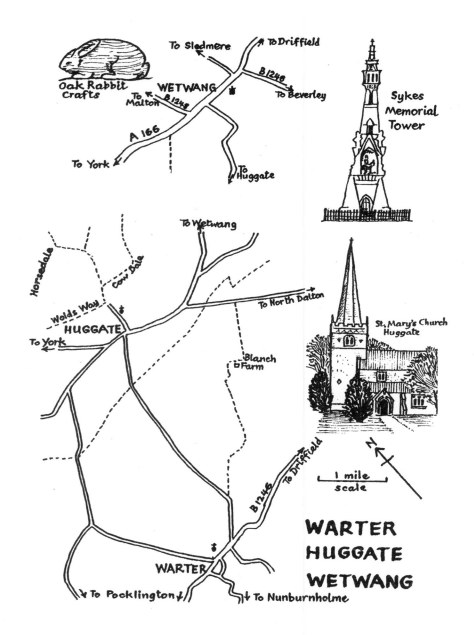

To Sledmere To Driffield

Oak Rabbit Crafts

WETWANG

B 1248

To Malton

B 1248

To Beverley

A 166

To York

To Huggate

Sykes Memorial Tower

To Wetwang

Horsedale

Cow Dale

Wolds Way

HUGGATE

To York

To North Dalton

Blanch Farm

St. Mary's Church Huggate

N

1 mile scale

B 1246 To Driffield

WARTER

To Pocklington

To Nunburnholme

WARTER
HUGGATE
WETWANG

WARTER, HUGGATE, WETWANG

Warter is a picturesque village in a valley of the Wolds, on the course of the old Roman road between Brough and Malton. An 1840 account refers to Warter as 'an indifferently built village' but in the 1850s and 60s the lord of the manor had most of the old buildings replaced by substantial brick dwellings, of various designs but apparently by the same architect, giving the place that air of comfortable well-being often acquired by an 'estate' village. You can see the stone carved figures showing the year of building on the walls of some of the houses. Close to the village green a few of the older houses remain.

By the site of the present church there was an Augustinian priory founded in 1132 but there are no visible remains. The name Warter Priory was adopted for the mansion in the park west of the village, a house which had its beginnings about 1700 but which was mainly Victorian. It has now been demolished. It had various owners, including from late last century the Wilson family of the Ellerman-Wilson shipping line. Charles Wilson became the first Lord Nunburnholme and members of the family are commemorated in elaborate carved monuments in St. James's church and in somewhat over-elaborate tombstones in the graveyard.

From the village green you approach the church, which stands on higher ground, along a grassy path between yew hedges.

Looking at the exterior of the church you may wonder, as I did, why the fabric looks slightly odd. It took me a minute or two to realise that it has been built of very small stone blocks, each about the size of a brick. The church door will probably be open and you may be interested to examine those monuments.

The village green is attractive and well maintained. The sun shone when last I stood by the war memorial and admired the contrasting colours of the laburnum blossom and yew foliage close to the much photographed row of thatched houses.

Pictures of these houses have appeared on countless 'beautiful Britain' calendars.

Just recently a friend of mine found them featured on a jig-saw puzzle in a shop in Skegness!

Maybe one day an enlightened local council or some benefactor will provide a seat or two for people spending a pleasant hour enjoying the picturesque scene.

The lane to Nunburnholme undulates between the fields and woodlands, has little motor traffic and provides an enjoyable walk with glimpses of a variety of birds. One May morning we watched several goldfinches as well as the more common chaffinches and warblers. Public footpaths into the country-side from the middle of Warter are non-existent. The most inviting dale, leading away north from beside the village pond, has a very firm NO ENTRY sign. But a little way out of the village you can find places to walk where no one will object. Half a mile or so up the road towards Minningdale and Huggate a path goes off to the right which takes you beside the wide fields and plantations, along the steep slopes of Lavender Dale, around Blanch Farm to the North Dalton - Huggate road. This walk is in typical Wolds country. You will need at least an hour to go gently from the one road to the other but, given a fine day, I think you will enjoy it.

Another way to see and appreciate

typical Wolds scenery is to walk from a point on the Warter–Huggate road about half a mile south of Huggate village. Have a look at this sketch map:

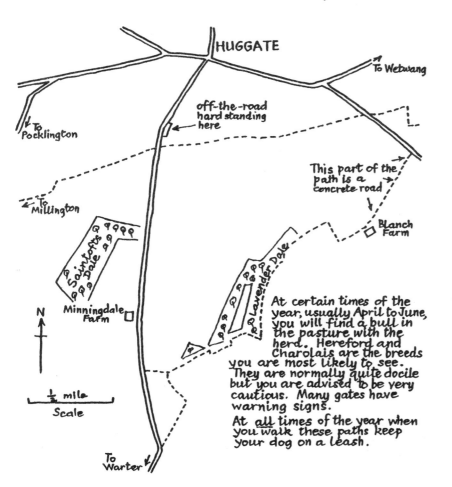

HUGGATE

To Wetwang

To Pocklington

off-the-road hard standing here

To Millington

This part of the path is a concrete road

Blanch Farm

Saintofts Dale

Lavender Dale

Minningdale Farm

N

½ mile
Scale

At certain times of the year, usually April to June, you will find a bull in the pasture with the herd. Hereford and Charolais are the breeds you are most likely to see. They are normally quite docile but you are advised to be very cautious. Many gates have warning signs.
At all times of the year when you walk these paths keep your dog on a leash.

To Warter

There is concrete hard standing in three places off the road – a relic of wartime tank training days and in surprisingly good condition – where you can leave a car. The track goes west to Millington Pasture and east nearly to Tibthorpe. Either way will provide you with fine views and plenty of interest. In the much improved grassland dropping away on the west to the woodland of Saintofts Dale there will probably be a herd of cattle; a change from the ubiquitous sheep. (See my note on the previous page about bulls). Barley flourishes on the far-reaching fields. Since the days of the enclosures there have been huge fields on these gently sloping chalklands. The hawthorn hedges you see are the original field boundaries and very few have been removed. The size of the fields provided a hard lesson for the young farm lads in the days of the working horses, as they learned to plough a straight furrow.

Stand and watch the wind's ripples on the corn. Through the growing season there are different colours, according to the kind of barley and the stage of growth; in some fields you will see a red-brown sheen across the young crop and in others a beautiful yellow-green. The wintertime landscape up here is equally attractive. Try walking these paths on a frosty morning and enjoy the exhilarating air. You get a marvellous sense of space as you go across the high parts of the wolds. The horizon curves away and there seems to be no end to the wide rolling vista of a hundred shades of white and green and brown. When you have left the road behind there is no distracting man-made noise to stop your enjoyment of the wolds' natural music.

'It soonds in t snarlin wind fra t sea
    at howls awaah ti t west,
It soonds in t breeze at gently hushes
    coontry sahde ti rest,
It soonds in t flootherin swaal o t leaves,
    in t rustlin swish o t corn

It soonds in t crawin of all t cocks in t
    staggarth ivvery morn;
An t bleeat o t lambs an t yows in t fields,
    in t songs o t bods an t bairns,
An t cattle comin ooam at neet, a lowin
    oot in t laanes.
All mak up t sweetest music at ti me
    all t coontry hawds,
Oor choruses o t hills an t daales, oor
    music ere on t wawds.'
Those lines are from the dialect poem
'Music on t Wawds' by Henrietta Blakeston.

"If there's an inch of snow down at Pocklington there'll be a foot at Huggate." An exaggeration, but with an element of truth. Looking from the west Huggate seems to sit in a saucer shaped depression in the wolds, gathering the breezes to itself and, in a severe winter, needing the services of the snow-ploughs rather more than other villages. Huggate has a pleasant village green, from which you can stroll in all directions; up to

48

the recently refurbished Wolds Inn, along to the village pond with its formidable fence and resident ducks, or down to the church. I expect you will find the church open so you can sign the visitors' book. Have a look at the boards on the wall beneath the tower, one of which has this notice:

> This spire was repaired in 1830 by T. Filey without scaffolding
> T. Cross
> J. Turner Churchwardens

I know that steeple-jacks sometimes work wonders with a few ropes and a ladder, but evidently the church wardens were especially impressed with Mr. T. Filey's skill. Or were they just astonished at his folly? I wonder, did Mr. T. Filey die peacefully in his bed, or was he finally spread eagled over some lofty buttress? I shall never know!

At the other end of the church is quite a different notice; an obituary appraisal of a previous Rector of Huggate.

TO THE MEMORY OF
THE REVᴰ JOHN WHALEY A.M.
38 YEARS RECTOR OF THIS PARISH
WHO DIED MAY 31, 1798, AGED 76
IN PRACTISE AS WELL AS PROFESSION
A TRUE MINISTER
OF
JESUS CHRIST.
ENDEARED TO HIS NUMEROUS FRIENDS
BY HIS
HUMILITY INTEGRITY & LIBERALITY;
AND BY HIS PARISHIONERS,
FOR HIS STRICT AND UNREMITTED CARE
OF THEIR BEST INTERESTS,
BOTH TEMPORAL AND ETERNAL,
REVERED, BELOVED AND LAMENTED
AS
AN INSTRUCTOR, A FRIEND & A FATHER.

"Thou good & faithful Servant!
"Enter into the Joy of thy Lord"

That seems to me to have a ring of sincerity and truth. The words have a splendid sonority. Stand there in the choir and try reading it all aloud.

We are not told who composed that tribute. The chances are that in 1798 a large proportion of the parishioners would not be able to read it. A 1961 study of some parish registers in the East Riding, directed by W.P. Baker of Leeds University, showed that in the decade 1791–1800 in, for example, Wetwang, 42 per cent of people married in church could not sign their names. The accomplished craftsman who sank the very deep well, 340 ft, on Huggate green (now sealed off but in use for many generations) signed the receipts for his payment by making a mark. His name was James Lollit and he was paid a total of 27 guineas by instalments between November 1766 and February 1767.

The Wolds Way comes down from Glebe Farm to the road going north from Huggate and you may like to follow it for a mile or so to the top of the steep slopes of Horsedale. Stand there by the stile and you have ancient earthworks stretching away to left and right,

embankments raised by Bronze Age and early Iron Age people about 2500 years ago, probably to define their boundaries. The Wolds Way continues down the slope into Holmdale and up to Fridaythorpe. Perhaps you could arrange to have your transport meet you there. Or you could go back towards Huggate and turn off to explore Cowdale to the east. The paths are marked with arrows and are easily followed. You will enjoy the peace of the dales and, if you wish, you can go all the way through the pastures beside the plantations and across the fields to the main road near Wetwang.

Above Cowdale the public right of way through the crops is kept clear by the use of herbicide

From this huge old ash tree in Cowdale, on the path from Huggate to Wetwang, another public path goes south-east to the road near Fox Covert Farm

People, (off-comed uns, frev awaah), hearing the name Wetwang for the first time, think it curious and ask its meaning. It is of Norse origin, I believe, and indicates wet land, though, apart from man made ponds, there is hardly any ground holding the rain water on these chalk wolds. Wetwang has had at least one clay-based pond for over a thousand years.

'At t name o Wetwang people starts
An thinks Ah cums fra foreign parts;
But we're all British reight enough —
A bit o real good Yorkshire stuff
Is t fowk at lives i Wetwang.

It's theer Ah larned ti foller t ploo,
Ti scruffle tonnups, milk t awd coo,
An theer Ah nearly rove mi shet
Oor maister's shays o corn ti get
Ti t staggarth doon i Wetwang.

An noo they're teachin me ti feight,
I uniform wi buttons breight;

Ah seer Ah gat a vast mair joys
I hankercher an corderoys
Mang farm lads doon i Wetwang.'

Those verses are from the poem 'Lahtle Wetwang' written by George Hardwick in 1916, the year of the death of another Wetwang dialect poet Moses Sowersby, a collection of whose work was published in 1914. Moses, who went blind at the age of 12, was one of the first pupils to attend class in the present school building which was erected at the expense of Tatton Sykes in 1843. (The building has been much altered since.) Before 1843 those Wetwang children who had any formal education at all went to a class in the church. The church of St. Nicholas is of Norman origin, with additions and alterations of various dates, and was restored early this century.

Round the church there are many old yew trees and just one oak, away in a corner of the graveyard, planted in memory of John Perrin Brown, the village doctor for 24 years up to the 1960s. He was a successor to the legendary Seth Tinsley who spent a lifetime meeting the medical needs of the wolds people of the Wetwang area.

Seth Tinsley, the 'Wolds Doctor' was reputed to be a very good judge of horses. He kept several himself.

(No doubt he would have had interesting things to say about my attempt to draw his pony!)

He travelled many thousands of miles on horseback or in his trap. It is said he only sent bills to those he thought could afford to pay. He never retired. He died in 1924 and is remembered as 'The Beloved Physician' on his gravestone close to the churchyard path.

Recent housing development has altered the shape of Wetwang village. For centuries it retained its one 'street' character, was little altered by the coming of the Malton to Driffield railway in the 1850s, or by its demise a century later. The name Station Hill is still there. The original street is part of the busy A166 road and half way along it are the premises of Oak Rabbit Crafts, where beautiful furniture is hand made of English oak.

English oak trunks are sawn and stacked with meticulous care for natural seasoning. Each board is left for at least a year for every inch of its thickness

The firm was established some twenty years ago by Peter Heap, who learned and practised his skills in the workshops of another well-known Yorkshire furniture maker. He is helped by his son and one other craftsman. Between them they produce oak furniture of great beauty as well as utility, each piece bearing the registered rabbit trade mark.

There may be an opportunity for you to see the craftsmen at work, but obviously you will not want to disrupt their routine unnecessarily.

About two miles north east of Wetwang and visible over a wide area of the wolds stands the Tatton Sykes memorial tower, erected in 1865. Built and carved in sandstone it has numerous S monograms, odd projections and various inscriptions. There is a relief of Sir Tatton on horseback and another of a plough with cottages behind. To my mind it has very little architectural merit, but you may disagree. At one time interested parties were allowed up the interior stairway to appreciate the view from 120 ft. above the fields, but that has not been possible now for many years. Formidable iron railings surround the base

of the tower and the gate is securely locked. Before you leave the Wetwang area you could go and see what you think of it.

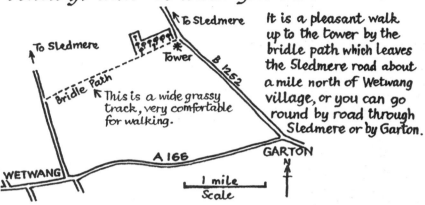

It is a pleasant walk up to the tower by the bridle path which leaves the Sledmere road about a mile north of Wetwang village, or you can go round by road through Sledmere or by Garton.

This is a wide grassy track, very comfortable for walking.

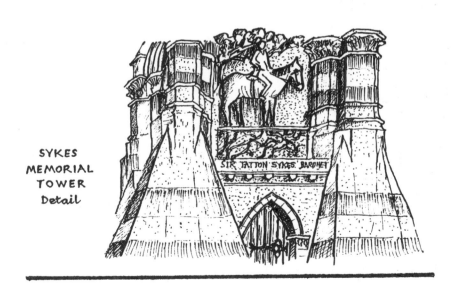

SYKES MEMORIAL TOWER Detail

SIR TATTON SYKES BARONET

6

SETTRINGTON WINTRINGHAM

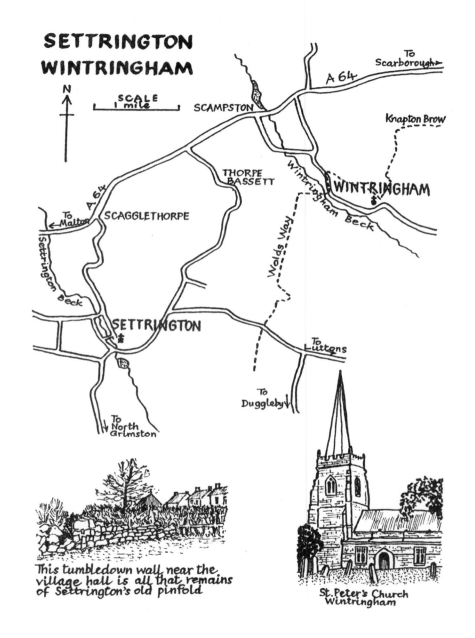

This tumbledown wall near the village hall is all that remains of Settrington's old pinfold

St. Peter's Church Wintringham

SETTRINGTON
WINTRINGHAM

Look around you as you walk the beckside paths through the middle of Settrington village in early summer and you will probably get the impression, as I did, that it is a village of prize-winning gardeners. Vegetables seemed unusually advanced and prolific; flowers bloomed in splendid variety and profusion. One lovely garden had an unusual big flower container— the funnel of a steam locomotive —and another had a strangely grafted fruit tree, the like of which I had never seen before.

There are three distinct parts to Settrington; the stone dwellings, mostly built about 1800, with their long gardens, facing but standing well back from the beck, the area of rather older houses and farmsteads beside Town Green to the west beyond the school, and the more recently erected houses between the beck and the road north to Scagglethorpe.

Beckside

Town Green

In addition the church and Settrington House, with its home farm beneath the wold, have the south end of the village to themselves, the other dwellings that were once there having been removed during the estate improvements carried out about 200 years ago.

You will enjoy strolling round. Architecturally almost all the buildings are pleasing. You should visit All Saints' Church which is usually open. A printed guide obtainable inside is very helpful.

The names of the rectors since the 13th century are displayed on a board and include Isaac Taylor (1829–1901) who lived here from 1875 to 1887. He was a brilliant scholar who wrote a number of books on his studies of the alphabet, of old languages and of place-names. He was known as 'the Darwin of English philology', being almost contemporary with Charles Darwin (1809–1882) whose theories and writings caused such controversy in Victorian England. His scholarship probably had little impact on the local community but he deserves to be much better known; we East Yorkshire people ought to be proud of our association with him. Earlier on the list of rectors occurs the name of Dr. Gilbert about whom an odd tale is told by Canon Cooper, the 'walking parson' of Filey who wrote about Yorkshire people and places. Gilbert was a dinner guest of Mark Masterman Sykes (who acquired the manor of Settrington on his marriage to Henrietta Masterman in 1795). It was the time of the Napoleonic wars. Sykes expressed the opinion that it was likely that Napoleon would be assassinated any day. He said that if someone gave him 50 guineas he would pay the donor a sovereign for every day of Napoleon's remaining life. Gilbert took the wager and became rich as Napoleon lived on and on. (A sovereign a day would have paid the wages of 10 or 12 of Sykes's estate workers) Eventually paying the dues became such a burden for Sykes that he made it the subject of a civil court action in London. Masterman Sykes died in 1823 and was succeeded by his brother Tatton. Canon Cooper thinks that the wager affair was the reason why Tatton Sykes never had any time for parsons!

Church of All Saints Settrington

Beyond the church the road to the hall is a private road. In this part of the village the trees are a great delight and if you pay a visit on a sunny day in early spring the beauty of the daffodil carpet will take your breath away. The old rectory is a fine building sharing the shelter of the beeches. Beside the beck the mill house has the date 1790 over its door. The mill ground corn up to the 1930s.

Settrington House

To appreciate the sight of the south front of the big house you have to stand on the roadside bank as you come down the hill from Settrington beacon. The grounds are beautifully maintained. A lake across the road is home for swans and coots and mallards. You can only admire from a distance; a closer approach is discouraged by the notice boards on tree trunks near the road: PRIVATE GROUNDS NO TRESPASSERS PLEASE. The PLEASE makes a change from the more usual threat of prosecution or the peremptory KEEP OUT.

The Masterman family built the present Settrington House in 1793 and pulled down its Elizabethan predecessor which had stood to the east of the church. Extensive renovation followed serious fire damage in 1963.

In the earlier house Lord Darnley, who was married at 20 years old to Mary Queen of Scots and murdered at 22, spent his childhood, being educated by his mother Margaret Lennox, a daughter of Henry VII, as a Roman Catholic claimant to the English throne. The Earl of Lennox had been given the Settrington estate by the Crown after it was forfeited by Francis Bigod, executed in 1537 for his part in the Pilgrimage of Grace. Not many people put forward Lord Darnley's residence as one of Settrington's claims to fame, as his character was certainly not one to be proud of. In his book 'England under the Tudors' G.R.Elton writes that Darnley 'combined in himself all the worst features of the Stuart character — stupidity, arrogance, moodiness, obstinacy, licentiousness, unreliability.' One wonders how he got as far as he did.

Elm Tree Farm
(without the elm tree)

Town Green now has none of the majestic trees which are so important a feature of the south end of Settrington but is none the less a very attractive place. In Colin Hayfield's intriguing book of old photographs ('Birdsall Estate Remembered' published in 1988) there are pictures of the ancient elm which gave Elm Tree Farm its name. It was taken down piecemeal as it became dangerous. Evidently it was a really tremendous specimen, but no trace remains.

As you approach Town Green on the road from Norton you pass an oak tree planted at the time of George VI's coronation in 1937. There are other commemorative trees beside the beck near the school; a lime for George V's silver jubilee in 1935, another for the present queen's silver jubilee in 1977.

For about 100 years, until 1958, Settrington had a railway station on the Malton to Driffield line. The station was south of the village on North Grimston lane and would save the farmers' horses a much longer haul with grain and other produce, but the Settrington people would not find it very convenient to use the passenger trains. From Town Green it would be almost as quick to walk to Norton as to the village station. Last century stone from the local quarries was transported by rail and the villagers were spared the sight and sound of the

thundering juggernauts which, since the quarries were brought into use again recently, have been going along narrow local roads which were made originally for much less demanding traffic.
Settrington station buildings have been converted into a private dwelling. A little way nearer the village a track to the east takes you to join a pleasant public beckside path to North Grimston. This is an enjoyable walk on fairly level ground and not too far to go there and back in an afternoon.

I think an even more enjoyable walk is from Settrington Beacon down to Wintringham. From the sixteenth century the beacon was one of the links in the East Yorkshire system of defence and it is still marked on the Ordnance Survey maps at a point about 200 metres above sea level on the road from Settrington to West Lutton. Plantations cover the high wold in that area now and the Wolds Way footpath crosses the road there on the way down to Wintringham. It was high summer when last I walked that way and in the middle of a heat wave I appreciated the shade of the larches and the beeches. It was quiet. The cooing of the wood pigeons was almost the only sound and, as Kathleen Stark wrote in her dialect poem about stockdoves; 'there's summat varry soothin iv a stoggy's gentle coo — it maks ye think o larch woods wi t gowld sunleet shinin through' (Wood pigeons and stockdoves alike are all stoggies in our vocabulary). I had no need to imagine the larch wood and the sunlight —they were there. It felt as if we, the stoggies and I, had the world to ourselves.

Emerging from a leafy tunnel, at the top of a steep chalk slope on your way north, pause for a minute or two to enjoy the view. I nearly wrote 'the magnificent view' but 'magnificent' is not really appropriate for that prospect of undulating pasture, woodland and farmland. 'Delightful' would be better. The track leaves Rowgate Farm on the left and joins an asphalted road with very wide grass verges full of wild flowers.  That July morning the pink and white blooms of the lesser bindweed made a beautiful ground cover close to the road. Butterflies by the hundred enjoyed them, with the scabious, the purple thistles and the rest. In the hedgerows there were yellowhammers. A leveret waited  until I was quite close before lolloping off in front of me. Beyond the hedges the greens of peas and beans alternated with the golds of the barley and the wheat

with here and there a patch of bright poppies in the ripening corn.

Approaching the western end of Wintringham village you cross the beck by a footbridge. If you have chosen a hot day you may be ready, as I was, to cool your feet.

The beck once provided power for two mills; Linton Mill, about a mile away, and Scampston Mill a little further downstream. Linton Mill no longer relies on water power but is a thriving concern producing animal foodstuffs. Scampston Mill went out of use in the 1930s, the wheelhouse is derelict and the mill pond overgrown. Mr. Aconley ("77 if I last till Christmas"), who farmed Scampston Mill Farm and still lives there, let me have a look around. He remembers when the mill was in working order, admires the skills of the old craftsmen who built it and is sad to see it in a state of decay.

Scampston Mill Farm dated from 1770

The mill wheelhouse is now derelict

Wintringham is surrounded by fine trees. There are extensive Forestry Commission plantations but I am thinking not of them but of the beeches, sycamores, oaks and Scots pines which abound in and around the village. The beeches near the gates to Place Newton, not far from the church, look down on a snowdrop carpet in February and the stately old Scots pines in the deer park are a joy at every season.

Deer Park Wintringham

The Wolds Way path goes round the back of the village to a point near the church before turning north up the wold through the conifers. You may wish to carry on walking that way to see the views north from Knapton Brow and Heslerton Brow, but find time to go the length of the village street to enjoy the picturesque chalk- and brick-built houses.

St. Peter's Church, the largest for miles around, is certainly worth a visit. There is some fine stained glass. The woodwork of the Jacobean pews and some of the carvings I found especially interesting and there is a 17th century memorial with an intriguing rhyming acrostic. The south door, studded with hundreds of old nails, is more noteworthy for its age than its beauty.

On our last visit we sat just beyond the churchyard to eat our sandwiches. We were thrilled by the company of a wren which moved quickly in and out of the bushes close by and approached within a couple of feet, without, it seemed, any fear at all. There was a robin, too, to share our picnic.

7

St. Christopher
Patron saint of travellers

15th century wall painting,
one of 'the saints of the
frescoes' in the Church
of St. Peter and St. Paul,
Pickering

PICKERING
NEWTONDALE

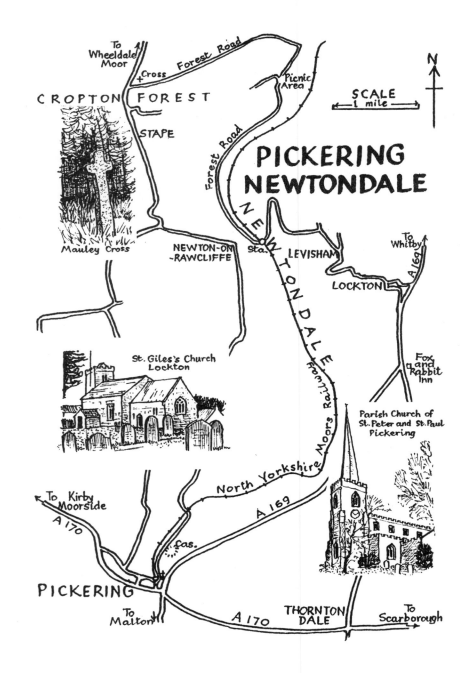

PICKERING NEWTONDALE

Pickering is on the western edge of the area I have defined as East Yorkshire and also, as an increasing number of tourists are becoming aware of its many attractions, on the edge of my 'lesser known' category. Describing some of the buildings in the town Nikolaus Pevsner writes 'Pickering is not architecturally rewarding.' There may be few structures of real distinction to delight a professional architect but to my eyes the whole place is pleasing and interesting, a mixture of styles and materials, old and new sitting happily side by side.

To explore Pickering properly you need at least a full day. I suggest that you begin in the parish church of St.Peter and St.Paul which stands prominently in

the middle of the town. Get a descriptive leaflet from the table near the south door and have a good look at the marvellous wall pictures, painted more than 500 years ago. They were covered over, then brought to light again and restored in Victorian times. They have been carefully looked after since. Sit in a pew and spend a few minutes enjoying the sight of one of our country's most complete sets of late medieval murals.

You will wish to look too at the monuments and memorials mentioned in your leaflet. Being interested in the history of rural and agricultural matters I was pleased to read the tribute to William Marshall, and to his brother John. The early 19th century obituary writers had a style of their own; brevity, even for a memorial tablet carved in marble, was evidently not regarded as a virtue. William was '—an excellent mechanic, had a considerable knowledge of most branches of science, particularly of philology, botany and chemistry, but was indefatigable in the study of Rural Economy. In his works are recorded the best practices of English Agriculturalists——'. William Marshall it was who founded England's first Agricultural Institute, in the building which was once his home in the middle of Pickering and which is now the Beck Isle Museum of Rural Life.

WILLIAM MARSHALL
OF SINNINGTON
PIONEER OF AGRICULTURE
1745-1818
LIVED HERE AND MODIFIED
THIS BUILDING TO MAKE
A COLLEGE OF AGRICULTURE
IN 1818

Beck Isle Museum   Pickering

I recommend that you spend an hour or so there. In the words of the Museum's descriptive booklet: '—the collection aims to reflect local life and customs and to trace many of the developments in social and domestic life during the last 200 years. Formality has been avoided—' To many of my generation some of the exhibits are reminders of a half forgotten childhood! When I see a dolly tub and a peggy stick as museum pieces I realise how hard my mother worked to get the weekly washing done!

Not so many years ago Pickering was a centre of railway activity. My 1907 Yorkshire guide book describes Pickering as ' a nicely situated town, the local greatness of which has not been increased by its abundant railway accommodation'. Being on the line from York to Whitby and having branches to Scarborough in the east and to Helmsley and the main line between York and Darlington in the west, it served a great many rural communities. One by one, from 1950, the railways were closed and dismantled. Only one stretch of line remains; that between Pickering and Grosmont, taken over, restored and operated by North

Yorkshire Moors Railway. (The story of the Whitby and Pickering railway line is very well told in David Joy's 'Dalesman' paperback of 1969. You may still be able to get a copy.) Steam-engine hauled passenger trains now run on a regular time table most days between March and early November. You can get all the information you need about the services from Pickering station. To travel between Pickering and Grosmont by train is an excellent way to enjoy the scenery of Newtondale. For well over a century the

Pickering Castle   King's Tower   Coleman Tower

line has had the reputation of being one of the most scenic in the country.

Your exploration of Pickering should include a visit to the castle. It is now looked after by English Heritage who have produced an excellent booklet to help you make the most of your visit.

Stand beside the King's Tower on top of the motte and look around. The castle still has enough of the remains of all the usual features of a mediaeval fortress for you, with a little imagination, to bring life and movement back into the scene and to see it as it was 500 years ago. Given an informed guide, children can learn more of 15th century English social history from a tour of Pickering castle than from half a dozen chapters in a text book.

Mill Tower from outside the gatehouse   Diate Hill Tower

John Leland, visiting Pickering about 1540 when the castle was falling into a state of disrepair, wrote '...the castelle waulles and the toures be meatly welle, the logginges yn the ynner court that be of timbre be in ruine...'. He had this to say about the town generally : 'The toune of Pykering is large but not welle compact togither. The greatest part of it with the paroch chirch and the castel is on the south est part of the broke renning thorough the toune, and standith on a great slaty hille. The other part of the toun is not so bigge as this : the brook rennith bytwixt them that sumtyme ragith, but it suagith shortely agayn; and a mile beneth the toun goith ynto Costey...'.   When, on a beautiful morning last summer, I leant on the parapet of the bridge near the Beck Isle Museum and looked at the quietly flowing beck on its way to join the Costa stream, it was difficult to imagine that it 'sumtyme ragith', though I know that to be true. The impression of peace and pleasantness that morning was enhanced by the brief presence of a kingfisher close to the bridge. A rare delight.

Rising on Lockton High Moor, the Pickering Beck flows the length of Newtondale, gathering on the way the waters of Levisham Beck which runs in the steep-sided valley between the villages of Lockton and Levisham. Lockton lies just west of the main Whitby road about 5 miles north of Pickering, a compact village of stone-built houses and farmsteads.

I suppose Lockton's population has rarely exceeded 300 people but it seems to have been well provided with places of worship. The church of St. Giles dates from the 1680s and just across the road is the large chapel erected for the Wesleyans early in the 19th century. I am told that until quite recently, on the other side of St. Giles's, there was another chapel for the Primitive Methodists.  That chapel has gone now and its site is incorporated into the space for new cottages (three of which I rejoice in the names of Lock, Stock and Barrel!) Have a look at the dignified simple interior of the church and read inside about its dedication to St. Giles.

Providing for three worshipping congregations in Lockton seems to me to be over anticipating the demand, even though the village people, up to Edwardian times anyway, probably found that meeting in church or chapel was their only opportunity to mix with friends and hear the news and gossip. There was sometimes rivalry between the elders of the chapels. I am reminded of the tale of a Wesleyan local preacher who, in his public prayers, regretted the decline in the numbers attending his chapel and went on to say "But we thank thee Lord that, while things are in a baddish way with us, they're worse off across at Prims."

The narrow road from Lockton to Levisham drops steeply down the valley side. Before driving that way I suggest you go the first few yards on foot and enjoy the view over the wooded dale; especially pleasing, I think, in autumn. You cross the beck and climb sharply up again to Levisham village, leaving the lonely

church of St. Mary forlorn in the beckside pasture below on your left. When that church was last in use for worship I do not know, though a headstone in the adjacent graveyard bears the date 1983. All the woodwork has gone, there are holes in the roof and the fabric seems to be deteriorating rapidly. The tower is home for a hundred pigeons.

The church of St. John the Baptist in the village was erected in 1884. The houses in Levisham stand back beyond the wide lawns of the road-side verges and make an attractive picture. If you continue past the inn, taking the road towards Levisham station, you come after about 600 yards to a sharp left turn. I suggest you take the track straight ahead. Further along you can conveniently leave your vehicle beside the track and put your walking shoes on. You are on the edge of excellent walking country. Beyond the stile near the gate ahead of you is a plaque which makes you welcome — provided, that is, that you leave your guns and tents, your fire lighters, metal detectors and vehicles behind.   You can obtain splendid views of Newtondale from several points on these moorland paths. The U-shaped valley is a very good example of the effects of glaciation, sculptured by a great glacier and the flow of its melt waters.

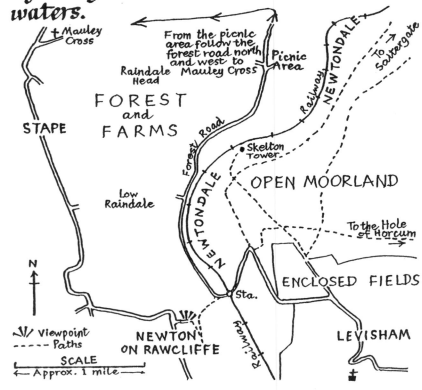

There is a wide choice of paths to walk in this beautiful stretch of countryside. Sheep graze freely and you should be careful to keep your dog under very close control. You could, if you feel really energetic and can make suitable transport arrangements, walk all the way to Saltergate or to the Hole of Horcum, but may be content just to go across to the edge of Newtondale near the remains of Skelton Tower and

watch the steam trains winding their way along the bottom of the valley. Skelton Tower was built about the middle of last century by the lord of the manor of Levisham, who was also rector of St. Mary's church there, as a private retreat. I cannot imagine what he wanted to retreat from, and should have thought that his own church, isolated from the village, was sanctuary enough.

Levisham station is about 1½ miles from Levisham village and, in the railway's busy period, may well have been used as much by the people of Newton-on-Rawcliffe as by those of Levisham. Though I should not envy the Newton housewife who had to carry her shopping bags up the path on the steep dale side. There is no access for any vehicles. Try climbing up there for yourself — and be rewarded by another wonderful panoramic view from the path just short of Newton village street.

From Levisham station you can take your vehicle a mile or so into Cropton Forest on a Forestry Commission road to a picnic area near Raper's Farm. Payment of a toll on this forest drive has recently been abolished. From the picnic area you can explore

the paths and enjoy the views over the dale.

Generally speaking, the younger conifer plantations offer a less desirable habitat for wildlife than more mature woodland. They lack light and they lack the variety of undergrowth. The valley where the railway runs in Newtondale has more bird and animal life than the higher areas of younger forest, but wherever you walk there are at least some signs and sounds of the natural life around you. Wood pigeons are commonly seen and heard; you may startle a jay into sudden chatter; at the edges of the scots pine plantations you will see piles of cone cores discarded by the grey squirrels which strip the cones to eat the soft centres and the seeds. In soft soil near the forest side or in the mud of wintertime look for creatures' footprints. In early summer listen for the tiny goldcrests which hang their beautiful nests near the end of spreading pine branches. And watch for the short-eared owl hunting for voles in daylight.

fox

ABOUT HALF SCALE

badger

To get back to the public road go north from the picnic area and follow the forest road round to Mauley Cross. This is one of the crosses in the area set up in mediaeval times as waymarks to help travellers on foot or horseback to choose the right direction over the moorland. There was a tradition that the traveller who reached a cross safely left a thanksgiving offering of coins, placed in a hollow on top of the monument, to be used eventually, one assumes, by some penniless traveller for his subsistence. To my delight, when last I felt in the hollow on Mauley Cross, I found the custom being maintained, though the cash was just a token and would certainly not have provided much in the way of board and lodging. (Nor, to be honest, would my own contribution!)

If you did not climb the bank up to Newton-on-Rawcliffe when you were at Levisham station, and so missed the panoramic view of the dale from the point I mentioned, pause in Newton village on your way home and enjoy it.

8

HALSHAM HOUSE

HILSTON
ROOS
HALSHAM

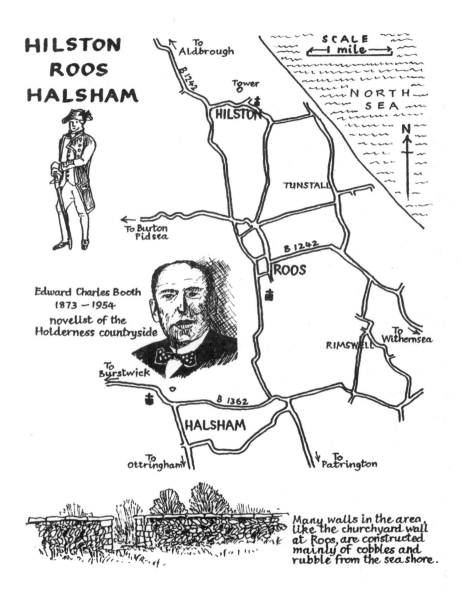

HILSTON
ROOS
HALSHAM

To Aldbrough

SCALE
1 mile

Tower

HILSTON

NORTH
SEA

N

TUNSTALL

To Burton
Pidsea

B 1242

ROOS

Edward Charles Booth
1873 — 1954
novelist of the
Holderness countryside

To Withernsea

RIMSWELL

To Burstwick

B 1362

HALSHAM

To
Ottringham

To
Patrington

Many walls in the area,
like the churchyard wall
at Roos, are constructed
mainly of cobbles and
rubble from the sea shore.

HILSTON, ROOS, HALSHAM

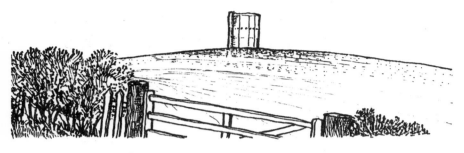

Admiral Storr's Tower stands on Hilston Mount, a mound to the north of Hilston village. It is about a mile from the sea and was erected in 1750 as a landmark, a navigational aid for ships in the area. It is 50 ft. high so its top is about 130 ft. above sea level and easily seen above the surrounding countryside. John Storr, who had the tower built, was the son of a Hedon magistrate who owned land at Hilston and who was buried there in 1752. John joined the navy and became an Admiral of the Red, a title which came from the British fleet's 17th century division into three squadrons, distinguished as red or centre, white or van

and blue or rear. There were originally only nine flag officers, admirals, vice-admirals and rear-admirals, but by the mid 18th century the organisation was changing and more flag officers were appointed.

Poulson's 1841 History of Holderness has a picture of the tower showing a flag flying, its chimney pots, its door and windows intact, railings round the base and a tidy path leading up to it. A newspaper picture in 1905 shows its walls almost covered with ivy and strengthened with tie rods. The description with the picture tells how the tower was 'inhabited by part of the (Storr) family during the building of the Hall in 1754 and used as a hospital for troops during an encampment on the coast in 1794/5.' I cannot imagine how any family could make much of a home in the limited space afforded by the tower, as each side of its octagonal shape measures barely 2 metres (though no doubt the admiral would be used to cramped quarters aboard his battleship!) nor can I think how it could be adapted as a 'hospital'.

In 1990 the tower stands lonely, slowly deteriorating amidst the crops, though the tie rods still hold the walls together and most of the brickwork remains sound. A stone carved plaque above the doorway is in fair condition still. The treads of the staircase in the semicircular section have fallen, the floors have gone and the door is rotting away. Long ago the windows were bricked up and the interior walls were adapted to make a pigeon cote. The dried out pigeon droppings accumulated to a depth of more than three feet and rabbits burrowed there. Elder bushes flourished inside. No longer is there a path to the tower, but you can see it easily from the road and it is likely to remain a landmark for several generations yet, (even without the flag of the Admiral of the Red!) John Storr was buried in Westminster Abbey in 1783. I should be interested to know how the title which he shared with flag-officer colleagues came to be given to one of the most beautiful of our butterflies.

Red Admiral

Hilston Hall, home of the Storr family from 1754, no longer exists but there is an attractive house on the site amid mature trees beside the road quite near the admiral's tower.

St. Margaret's Church at Hilston is a modern structure built in the 1950s to replace the Victorian church which was

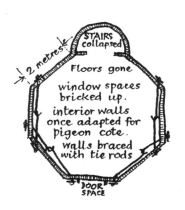
STAIRS collapsed
2 metres
Floors gone
window spaces bricked up.
interior walls once adapted for pigeon cote.
walls braced with tie rods
DOOR SPACE

Stone plaque with 'three storks proper', presumably the Storr family coat of arms, still in the tower wall above the door space.

St. Margaret's Church Hilston

almost completely destroyed by a bomb
jettisoned by a German bomber being
chased on its way home from a raid in 1942.
You can still see bomb-shattered gravestones in the churchyard. Stones from the
Norman arch of one of the doorways of the
original church were reused in the new
building's south door.

My old East Riding directory tells
me that in 1841 Hilston had 'only 43 souls
and 530 acres of land'. An 1890 account
tells of 552 acres 'inclusive of the beach'.
I suppose ownership of the beach was a
matter of importance when sand and
boulders and cobbles were much used in
the local buildings. Like most of the
Holderness coastline, the clay cliffs near

Hilston are being gradually eroded by the sea
and the 552 acres of 1890 cannot be taken
as an accurate figure a century later.
The road to Tunstall takes you almost to
the cliff edge so you can go that way to
enjoy a breath of sea air. Take great care
on the cliff top. It is this stretch of coast
which is featured in Winifred Holtby's
'South Riding' and also in the first of
Edward Booth's Holderness novels 'The Cliff
End'

Crumbling cliffs near
Hilston, south of
Aldbrough, which
Booth called Ullbrig.

(See the bibliography
for details of Booth's
Holderness novels)

Booth's stories are not nearly so well known
as I think they deserve to be. Anyone wanting
to learn more about the Holderness village
people and their environment a hundred years
ago could do no better than read his tales.
All around Hilston, Roos and
Halsham is intensively cultivated farmland.

Vistas have changed a great deal over the last 50 years as farming practices have changed. Old farm buildings, no longer meeting the farmer's needs, have been put to new uses or replaced by modern, quite different, structures which often stand stark against the skyline and fit less than comfortably into their surroundings.

You are more likely to see something like this, than this →

Technically no doubt the modern buildings are all that is required, scientifically designed for special purposes and made of economically sensible, readily available, materials. But to my eye they have none of the scenic attraction of the old style farm buildings and do not appear to be particularly durable. On the next page I have sketched the lay-out of a typical

family mixed farm of about 1800, before the age of farm machinery. As you move around the countryside near the coast take a closer look at the farmsteads; see if any of the old traditional buildings remain and if any of them were constructed with stone and cobbles from the shore.

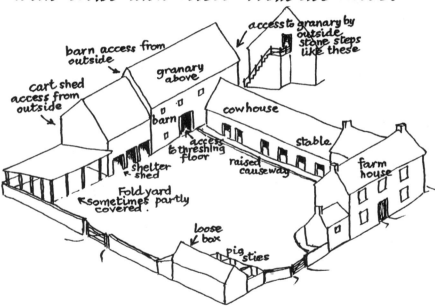

access to granary by outside stone steps like these

barn access from outside

granary above

cart shed access from outside

cowhouse

barn

access to threshing floor

stable

shelter shed

raised causeway

farm house

Fold yard sometimes partly covered.

loose box

pig sties

My friend Ron Wray has farmed all his life in this part of Holderness and lives here still. He knows that change is not always desirable progress. Ron has a keen interest in the language of his native country-side and has many times put his thoughts into dialect verse. These lines are part of one of his poems published in 1976 :

'Bridges an stiles — they ha'e vanished,
Oor feeatpaths ha'e melted away.
Awd kissin geeate's tummled ti pieces
An lane-lettin's gone oot tiday !
Gone are the banks of mah childhood
Wheer primrose an violet grew,
Gone are oor sweet-smellin hedges
Under the heel o the ploo !
The paddocks wheer Ah used ti wander
Sae happy, contented an blythe,
Are wide oppen desolate places
Wheer wind's harsh as the bite ev a scythe.
We've nowt ti be prood on, we mortals,
We'll ha'e nowt ti show for oor sweat ;
In the naame o progress we plunder—
An Ah knaw we're not hawf finished yet !'

   Ron goes on to deplore people's apparent lack of interest in conservation but also records his pleasure at seeing a newspaper picture of a girl planting trees. Each one of us should plant at least one tree for every year of our age. How do you stand on that score ?

   In spite of continuing change there is a great deal to be enjoyed in the Holderness landscape, especially, I find, on a bright day in autumn when the colours of the recently disturbed soils and the new sprouting corn are seen against a background of mature trees. I cannot match Edward Booth's literary skill in describing the scenery ; I can only urge you to take the time to stand and look for yourself. At Roos, for instance, the trees on the little eminence of Cruikham Hill, where the road south crosses Roos Drain, make a pleasing profile above the ploughland. There are paths between crops and drainage channels in this area, one of which is shown on the Pathfinder map going from Roos church all the way to Rimswell, but I found some difficulty in following them without going on cultivated ground.

The Victorian school building at Roos has been converted for dwellings. The modern school is beside the main street about 400 yards to the north.

The Roos parish register records the burial in 1654 of John Bottomley, 'scolemaster and scrivener,' so evidently Roos had some sort of a school in the early part of the 17th century. In the 19th century Charles Silversides 'taught the village school from 1844 to 1894...... a man who has left no memorial save the gradual extension of literacy and education in a remote rural society.' I am quoting from J. Lawson's 1959 account 'Primary Education in East Yorkshire 1560-1902'. This century too has seen a long serving schoolmaster in Roos having a lasting influence on his pupils. 'Gaffer' Bill Wilbraham is remembered with respect by, amongst very many others, former pupils David Eldred and John Boynton whom I met briefly at Hilston. John was in Burma for some years in wartime and he recalls with pleasure how Mr. Wilbraham wrote him regular letters.

There has been a church at Roos since the eleventh century. The Domesday survey of 1086 records 'a priest and a church and 30 acres of meadow'. Much of the present building dates from the 15th century. Extensive renovation was carried out in the 1840s when the porch at the west end was added. The yew trees beside the path also date from that time. The 15 steps from path to porch help to make the view of this end of the church more impressive.

The fabric of much of the church is rubble and cobbles from the sea shore. The variegation of colour in the stones, with the addition of small pieces in the mortar between them, makes for a very attractive surface when seen in the sunlight.

An unusual feature of Roos church is the stair turret rising above the roof from the vestry. You can see it best from the present day burial ground to the north east.

Have a look too at the interesting modern monument close to the road near the churchyard gate. It commemorates the life of Frank Hinch who gave money for improvements to the church.

For several generations after the Norman conquest the de Ros family had a castle on a site just south of the church. The only traces of its existence now visible are low mounds in the pasture below the churchyard. You may be able to make out the line of the moat which was partly excavated last century. The Roos estate changed hands a number of times over the years and in the 18th century was acquired by Mark Kirby of Hull, whose daughter married Richard Sykes of Sledmere. Subsequently two members of the Sykes family served for long periods as rector here.

For nearly 500 years Halsham was the home of the famous Constable family. Their house, which was close to the church, has now gone but their mausoleum, a round temple in the classical style, has dominated the local landscape for close on 200 years. It stands at the end of an avenue of yews across the road from

Halsham House, a beautiful Elizabethan brick building which was originally a free school and almshouse, founded by one of the Constables in 1579. It has a backcloth of the fine trees which almost hide All Saints' Church from the view of passers by on the road. Some parts of the church building are much older than others and the whole fabric is a mixture of dressed stone, rubble and brickwork, interesting but not particularly attractive.

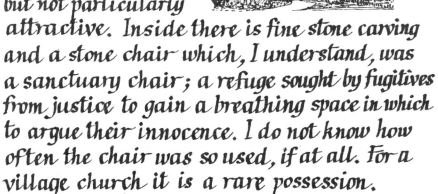

Inside there is fine stone carving and a stone chair which, I understand, was a sanctuary chair; a refuge sought by fugitives from justice to gain a breathing space in which to argue their innocence. I do not know how often the chair was so used, if at all. For a village church it is a rare possession.

The novelist Edward Booth was familiar with all the countryside around Halsham and used his knowledge of local people to give authenticity to the characters in his stories. A late Victorian priest at Halsham, I am told, had many of the attributes of Father Mostyn, a leading character in 'The Cliff End', described by J.B.Priestley as 'a magnificent creation and surely one of the liveliest and most attractive High Church parsons in all English fiction.'

There are few houses in the vicinity of Halsham church; the community consists mainly of farmsteads spread over a wide area. Walk by the Southside Road to East End and beyond on the Withernsea Road; see how many of the farm buildings have been altered to meet modern requirements, without entirely losing their character.

9

WANSFORD
TO THE SEA

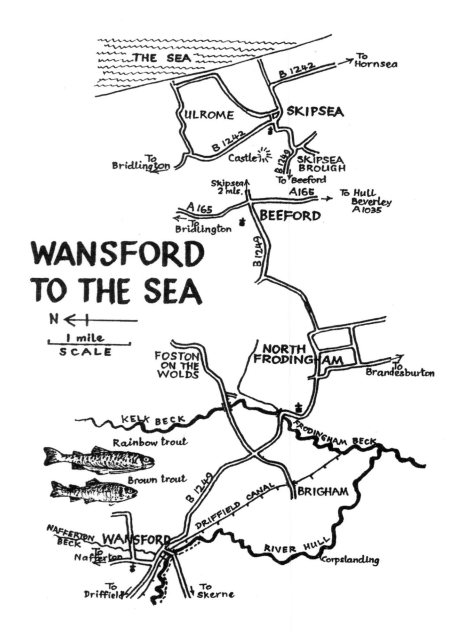

WANSFORD TO THE SEA

The old lock at Wansford

The fisherman near the old lock on the Driffield canal at Wansford looked the picture of contentment. The occasional noise of traffic on the road behind him disturbed him not at all. The whole scene on a very still morning last October was one of complete tranquility. You will often see fishermen at Wansford; the canal, the river Hull and the Nafferton beck all attract them. There are trout farms close by and The Trout Inn meets the needs not only of the fishermen but of discerning diners from afar.

It is about 50 years now since commercial craft last used the Driffield canal but it was busy for several generations from the 1770s and continued to meet some local needs even after the railways to and from Driffield were well established. It was cut originally because the navigation of the river Hull above Corpslanding was so difficult.

Close beside the old lock at Wansford, standing between canal and road, opposite the Manor House, is a very old and very big hollow oak tree. It must have been there for several hundred years and probably was already in its old age when the navvies were digging out the lock in the 1760s. I am pleased that they spared it and that no one's zeal for 'improvement' has since caused it to be removed; it remains an interesting and picturesque feature for us to enjoy.

Bridges on the Skerne road from

Wansford cross the canal and the river which here run close together. Immediately over the river bridge you can take a public path through the pasture  in either direction if you wish to walk beside the river. There is a public footpath too following the course of the Nafferton beck north from Wansford.

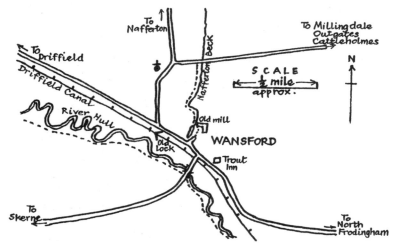

The path sign post beside the main road seems to point directly into the private garden of the old mill, but if you go round

This mill, on the Nafferton Beck, ground corn up to about 1920. Some 200 yards away, on the River Hull there was another mill, now demolished, which operated until the 1890s.

to the left of the building there is another direction arrow and access over the old mill race to the beck bank. Stand for a minute or two looking into the beck near the mill; you are almost sure to see fine trout lurking.

The church of St. Mary at Wansford was built in 1868 to the design of G.E.Street who also was the architect for the nearby parsonage and school (now converted for dwellings) which were erected in the 1870s. The three buildings together make an interesting group, with, to my eye, the intricate brickwork of the school house and parsonage being more attractive than the masonry of the church. See what you think. There are fine trees around.

A road goes east from near the church to rather isolated farmsteads on Nafferton Carrs. I like the names on the signpost and am intrigued by some of the other names of features in the locality like Kelk Lynesykes, Snakeholm, Pitwherry Nook and Cowslams Lane. No doubt they all had meaningful origins. It is Cowslams Lane that leads to Foston-on-the-Wolds after you have turned left off the Frodingham road from Wansford. On the subject of names — however did Foston acquire the 'on-the-Wolds' designation? Although on ground slightly higher than the surrounding carrs the village is many miles from the Wolds.

Cruckley Farm is on Cowslams Lane. Rare breeds of sheep and pigs and other animals are kept there and, during the summer months, there are regular open days on which members of the public can visit. Just beyond Cruckley Farm, on a little eminence on your right, are the remains of a windmill which is within 200 yards of an old watermill on Foston Beck. The road crosses the beck at Sheepdike Bridge, beyond which you can turn right and go down to the beckside path and the site of a brewery which is now the farmhouse and buildings of Brewery Farm. Brewery and mill were busy places through the nineteenth century and could be reached up the beck by commercial craft from the River Hull. A fire in the 1890s effectively ended the mill's useful life. The beck was being cleared of weeds when last we walked that way. Have a look at the unusual footbridge crossing the beck near Brewery Farm.

The bridge consists of one huge baulk of timber more than 50 ft. long, previously used, apparently, in some big building.

The stones from the graveyard close to St. Andrew's Church at Foston have been removed, to lean against the outside walls. A well trimmed lawn now occupies the space between road and church. One of the memorial tablets, on the south side of the tower, is a reminder of the time, not really so very long ago, when expectation of life was limited indeed. One son and three daughters of James and Fanny Bottrill died in the 1820s and 30s at the age respectively of six weeks, three years, six months and four years. The modern well designed churchyard entrance, with a seat, also commemorates someone whose life was short, and an infant remembered as 'a small bright spark of life.'

For me the most interesting feature of the church interior is a modern stained glass window in the north aisle with lovely flowers in a garden and a colourful saintly lady. We saw it illuminated by the mid day sun shining through the windows high on the south side and thought it beautiful.

Leaving the road near the church two public paths, sign posted but evidently little used, lead into the fields. One goes south east beside the beautifully kept garden, lawns and paddocks of Field House Farm and leads through the crops eventually to the Beeford road. After the first few hundred yards the going gets difficult and you may wish to retrace your steps. To follow the other path you start by opening a door in a wall to walk through a lovely cottage garden before going west beside the hedges towards Foston Beck. Again after a while you may find that the path is partly overgrown but it is very pleasant on a fine day to stroll even a little way in those quiet fields.

Back across the Wansford–Frodingham road and close to the canal is Brigham, a settlement of several farmsteads close together. You can enjoy a quiet canal side walk for quite a long way south from the bridge and maybe watch the activities of the members of Brigham sailing club who have their craft moored on the canal.

Along the road towards the sea you come to Frodingham church soon after crossing the beck, some distance from the village.

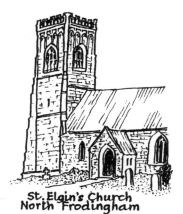

St. Elgin's Church
North Frodingham

Church Farm, with some of its structure dating from the 17th century, stands in the shadow of the church. Look at its finely built old brick chimney stacks.

Church Farm, North Frodingham

The church tower has unusually large bell openings. No doubt when the bells are rung they will be heard for many miles across the gently rolling countryside and across the level carrs. Bell ringing—'the exercise', as I believe the art is known to its adherents—is not so widely practised as it used to be. Not so often, to use John Clare's words, do we on the sabbath

'—hear once more the pleasant chiming bells
That from each steeple peeping here and there
Murmur a soothing lullaby to care'

nor do we nowadays often meet the like of Clare Ellin's old ringer who

'—one boot in the stirrup,
A sally i auther hand,
Chimes three bells on Sundays—
An, by gaw, they deea soond grand!'

Most of the Frodingham church-goers have a fair walk to service from the village. It is likely that the dwellings of the original village clustered near the church and bridge but over the years were moved to better drained sites to the east.

old market cross, North Frodingham

When this sketch was made in 1989 the cross was scheduled for restoration. It may not look quite like this any more.

Until late in the 18th century Frodingham had a weekly market but it lost its importance as Driffield grew.

Like Frodingham, Beeford is a 'street' village with most of its houses and farmsteads strung along both sides of a single street. There has been additional housing development near the cross roads at the eastern end of the village. As in so many places the church, with its

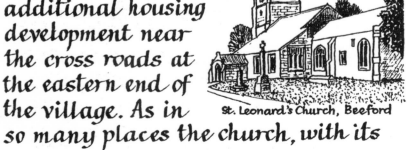
St. Leonard's Church, Beeford

splendid 15th century tower, is the most interesting building in the village. The old gravestones have been resited around a wide expanse of mown grass to the south of the church.

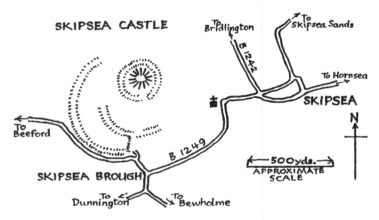

At Skipsea Brough you can walk round the mounds which are the remains of the Norman castle built by Drogo, lord of Holderness, late in the 11th century and demolished less than 200 years later. The story is that Drogo brought about the death of his wife, a niece of William the Conqueror, and had to run away. He was never captured.

A later overlord of Holderness rebelled against King Henry III who ordered that the castle be destroyed.

I marvel at the tremendous volume of earth which was moved to raise the motte which is extensive and about 35 ft. high. The labourers only had hand tools and primitive ox carts. Most of the material would be carried on hods and litters. (I wonder when wheelbarrows first came into use!)

All Saints' Church at Skipsea stands on slightly higher ground between the castle and the village. As at Beeford, most of the old headstones in the almost

All Saints' Church
Skipsea

circular graveyard have been relocated and an open space created between church and church-yard wall. Some of the gravestones now form an area of paving below the church tower. Again, cobble and rubble from the beach, less than a mile away, were used in the church building, and in a great many other buildings in Skipsea, too, as you will see when you walk through the village.

This building near the churchyard gate at Skipsea is one of many in the area in which cobbles have been used as well as bricks.

This chapter is headed 'Wansford to the Sea' so, to finish it properly, why not go to Skipsea Sands and enjoy a walk on the beach before you go home? Take the dog!

10

Looking over Troutsdale to Langdale Rigg

BROMPTON-BY-SAWDON
WYKEHAM FOREST
TROUTSDALE

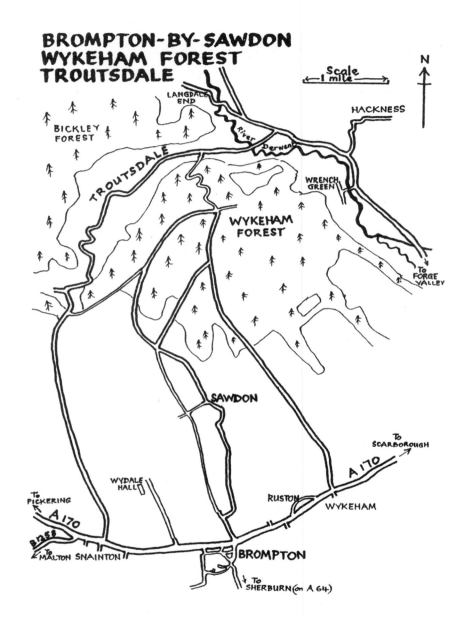

BROMPTON-BY-SAWDON
WYKEHAM FOREST   TROUTSDALE

Of all the places mentioned in these ten 'lesser known' East Yorkshire localities only one, Brompton-by-Sawdon, is featured in the Oxford Literary Guide to the British Isles. Brompton's claim to inclusion is simply that, in 1802, William Wordsworth was married in All Saints' Church there. Mary Hutchinson, who became his wife, lived at Gallows Hill Farm, a mile or so away from the village on the way to Scarborough, where she was house-keeper for her uncle. A framed copy of the banns and marriage certificate is kept in the vestry. That copy is not publicly displayed but there is, besides, much of interest in the church. As you go in have a close look at the south

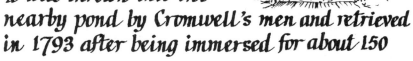

door, itself a fascinating piece of history. It dates from the 15th century and was formerly in the original nave, now the north aisle. It was thrown into the nearby pond by Cromwell's men and retrieved in 1793 after being immersed for about 150 years.

A recently prepared leaflet, of which copies are readily available on a table just through the door, tells you the church's story and describes the various features. Some of the windows are especially interesting, as are other memorials to members of the Cayley family, which has been prominent in the area for more than 450 years.

The church gates commemorate Sir Kenelm Cayley, who died in 1967, and are reached up an unusual sloping approach made, like most of Brompton's buildings, of locally quarried stone.

Springs in the grounds of Brompton Hall, close to the church, feed the fish pond into which the church door was thrown all those years ago. One pond leads to another and that in turn supplies, over a four-foot waterfall, the becks which cross the green, called the Butts, in the southern part of the village. A public footpath from the church to the Butts goes beside the ponds. The trees close by are a joy, especially some huge sycamores. Wordsworth wrote of a 'brotherhood of venerable trees.' Perhaps he was thinking of Brompton when he

'... heard a stockdove sing or say
His homely tale this very day;
His voice was buried among trees....'

It is a pleasure to wander around the Butts and watch the ducks and the geese, the moorhens and the coots. There is plenty of other bird life too. We had great delight in the presence of several goldfinches one day in the early autumn.

Brompton-by-Sawdon village school had its centenary in 1978 when a full account of its history to the end of the second world war was compiled. Close beside the school building, just across the little car park, springs feed the mill-pond below with crystal clear water. It is now a lifetime since the mill ground corn. The picturesque mill stream flows south and eventually joins the River Derwent.   Enjoy a walk around; the buildings are all interesting and well worth looking at.

Brompton Hall is now a school. It retains the original splendid stone gate-posts at its entrance and they are matched across the main road by a similar pair at the opening to Brompton Dale. The PRIVATE notice on

the gate cancels the implied invitation of the nearby open wicket gate and you will have to content yourself with looking at, rather than walking on, this historic stretch of East Yorkshire's countryside. Over this dale, in 1852, took place the world's first ever flight made by a fully grown man in a heavier than air machine. George Cayley of Brompton, later described by the president of the French Aeronautical Society as 'the incontestable forerunner of aviation, whose name should be inscribed in letters of gold on the first page of the aeroplane's history', whose pioneering work was acknowledged by the Wright brothers, had applied his remarkable brain to the problems of aviation for almost sixty years. In an essay on aerial navigation as long ago as 1809 he had clearly defined those problems. He was 79 years old when his flying machine carried his coachman over Brompton Dale. (The story goes that the coachman promptly gave notice—he was hired to drive, not fly!)

Sir George Cayley, Bt.
1773 – 1857
'The father of the aeroplane'

George Cayley was a gentle soul, a lover of peace. He would have been horrified at the later military use of mechanical flight. His inventive genius was not confined to the study of aviation. In 1804 he initiated a system of drainage for the Derwent floodland south of Brompton which has remained effective to the present time. Embankments were made along the river, far enough from the natural banks and high enough to contain the largest known floods of the area. The soil for these embankments was taken from deep trenches dug outside them, the trenches acting as drains for the surface water.

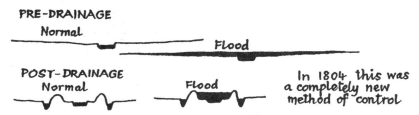

PRE-DRAINAGE
Normal
Flood

POST-DRAINAGE
Normal
Flood
In 1804 this was a completely new method of control

If eventually you go home from Brompton by the road to Sherburn on the A64, pause as you cross the river and you will see this system in operation.

George Cayley was probably responsible for more innovations and inventions than any other Englishman of his generation. He designed and produced finned missiles at the time of the threat of Napoleonic invasion. He perfected artificial limbs, designed a light weight bicycle wheel, invented the caterpillar tractor and worked on aspects of railway safety.

If you take the road going north from Brompton, through Sawdon, you are quickly into Wykeham Forest and soon come to a cross roads where, on the brow of the hill overlooking Troutsdale, there is a picnic place and space to leave your car.

From here you can enjoy walking on the tracks amongst the trees in any direction. The 1:25000 O.S. map is helpful. Some people consider the Forestry Commission's plantations to be uninteresting but I think that if they took the trouble to find out more about the different species of trees, to understand the purposes of the foresters' work throughout the seasons, they would get much pleasure from their forest walks.

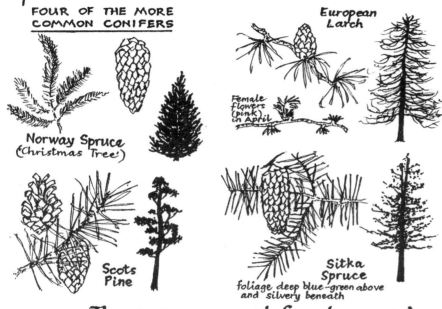

FOUR OF THE MORE COMMON CONIFERS

European Larch

Female flowers (pink) in April

Norway Spruce (Christmas Tree)

Scots Pine

Sitka Spruce
foliage deep blue-green above and silvery beneath

There are several forest nurseries not far from where you left your car. It is well worth going to have a closer look. Continuous research and experiment have established techniques for providing millions of strong seedlings of a variety of species to suit the different types of soil. The seeds come from many sources. I was astonished to read that the seeds of some conifers are so tiny that up to 50,000 young trees can be grown from just 1 lb. of, for example, Sitka spruce seed. The origins and progress of all the plants are very carefully recorded.

Before you leave the picnic area enjoy the view to the north towards Langdale Rigg. Just beyond the trees to your right is the isolated farm called Mount Misery. How it came to have that name you can decide for yourself. Mount Misery is just one of the rather lonely farmsteads which you will see along the length of Troutsdale, reached by tracks leading from each side of the winding road.

Go down the road in front of you and at the bottom of the hill turn left. In fine weather you will not wish to hurry through this dale; there is a pleasing prospect round every bend. I imagine that the people who live in the isolated farms will have to be entirely self sufficient; the nearest village communities are Hackness and Snainton, several miles away.

At the roadside near Troutsdale Lodge is the old schoolroom, now decaying. The decorative cross on the gable made me think it was a chapel, but I was wrong. Christabel Burniston, whose father was one of a large family living at the head of the dale in the 1880s, told me of the children's daily six miles walk to and from school.

Last September we had a picnic just off the road at a point south of the old school, before you come to Manor House, (Pt. 178 on the O.S. map) where a track leads up to Troutsdale Moor. A public footpath goes through the roadside plantation, amongst the blackberries, broom and bracken, to the heather covered moor, which in turn gives way to the conifers of Bickley Forest. If you enjoy a few minutes in a beautiful setting, completely cut off from civilisation's noises, this is a walk you should take.

Just past the buildings of Troutsdale Mill, where it is still easy to see evidence of the mill's working days, you climb the winding hill to another picnic place and viewpoint near Cockmoor Hall. Look back at the beautiful dale. Look, too, at the old earthworks nearby, which to me are something of a mystery. They date probably from Anglian times. If defensive what was being defended? If marking boundaries why are they so close together?

The road back to Snainton and Brompton is much less picturesque than that through Troutsdale, but enjoy your journey home.

BIBLIOGRAPHY

ALLISON K.J.   The East Riding of Yorkshire   Hodder &
                 Landscape   Stoughton
                                                   1976

                 East Riding Water mills   East Yorkshire
                                                   Local History
                                                   Society 1970
                                                   (E.Y.L.H.S.)

(Full list of E.Y.L.H.S. publications, and details
about membership, can be obtained from
The Secretary, % Beverley Library, Champney Rd.,
Beverley, HU 17 9BQ.)

BADDELEY M.J.B   Yorkshire   Nelson
                 Thorough Guide Series   1907

BAKER W.P.   Parish Registers and   E.Y.L.H.S.
                 Illiteracy in East Yorkshire   1961

BOOTH E.C.   Holderness novels:

                 The Cliff End   Grant Richards
                                                   1908
                                                   Putnam
                                                   1956
                 The Doctor's Lass   Grant Richards
                                                   1910
                                                   Putnam
                                                   1956
                 Fondie   Duckworth
                                                   1916
                                                   Putnam
                                                   1956
                 The Tree of the Garden   Duckworth
                                                   1922
                                                   Putman
                                                   1956
                 Kith and Kin   Duckworth
                                                   1929

BROADBENT I.E.   Portrait of the Yorkshire   Hale
                 Ouse   1982

BROWNE H.B   The Story of the East Riding   Brown
                 of Yorkshire   1912

COOPER A.N.   Curiosities of East Yorkshire   Brown

COWLEY W. (Ed.) An East Yorkshire Anthology   Yorkshire
                                                   Dialect Society
                                                   1965

(Full list of Yorkshire Dialect Society's
publications from The Hon. Librarian,
Y.D.S., School of English, The University,
Leeds. LS2 9JT)

DUCKHAM B.F.   The Yorkshire Ouse,   David &
                 The History of a   Charles
                 River Navigation   1967

                 The Inland Waterways   E.Y.L.H.S.
                 of East Yorkshire   1973
                 1700 — 1900

EDLIN H.L. (Ed.) North Yorkshire Forests   H.M.S.O
                 (Forestry Commission Guide)   1972

FAIRLIE G. and   The Life of a Genius   Hodder &
CAYLEY E.   Stoughton
                                                   1965

HALLIDAY W.J. and The White Rose Garland   Dent
UMPLEBY A.S. of   1949
The Yorkshire Dialect
Society (Eds.)

HAYFIELD C.   Birdsall Estate Remembered
                                                   Springhill
                                                   Pubns. 1988

HOLTBY W.   South Riding   Collins
                                                   1936

JOY D.   Whitby and Pickering   Dalesman
                 Railway   1969

KIGHTLY C. and   Lords of the City   York City
SEMLYEN R. for   The Lord Mayors of York   Council
York City Council and their Mansion House   1980

LAWSON J. — Primary Education in East Yorkshire 1560–1902 — E.Y.L.H.S. 1959

MEE A. — The King's England – Yorkshire, East Riding with York — Hodder & Stoughton 1964

NEAVE D. — East Riding Friendly Societies — E.Y.L.H.S. 1988

PEVSNER N. — The Buildings of England Yorkshire : York and the East Riding — Penguin 1972

Yorkshire : The North Riding — Penguin 1966 (reprint 1981)

RATCLIFFE R. — The Wolds Way – Long Distance Footpath Guide No. 12 — H.M.S.O for the Countryside Commission

SMITH L.T.(Ed.) — The Itinerary of John Leland 1535–1543 — Bell 1907

WHITE W. — History of the East and North Ridings of Yorkshire — White 1840

WOODWARD D. (Ed.) — Descriptions of East Yorkshire – Leland to Defoe — E.Y.L.H.S. 1985

GLOSSARY OF DIALECT WORDS

lane-lettin	the system under which small holders acquired grazing and hay-making rights on the wide verges of public lanes.
off-comed uns frev awaah	strangers from away
scruffle	cultivate between rows of growing crops
shavs	sheaves
staggarth	stackyard
swaal	swirl, throw
yows	ewes